And God
Smiled

© 2012 by Barbour Publishing, Inc.

Print ISBN 978-1-62029-153-5

eBook Editions:
Adobe Digital Edition (.epub) 978-1-62029-548-9
Kindle and MobiPocket Edition (.prc) 978-1-62029-547-2

Published by Barbour Publishing, Inc., P.O. Box 719, Uhrichsville, Ohio 44683, www.barbourbooks.com

Our mission is to publish and distribute inspirational products offering exceptional value and biblical encouragement to the masses.

ecpa Member of the
Evangelical Christian
Publishers Association

Printed in the United States of America.

And God
Smiled

**Simple Stories to
Warm Your Heart**

BARBOUR
PUBLISHING

God's gifts put man's best

dreams to shame

ELIZABETH BARRETT BROWNING

$\mathcal{A}$ smile is a universal sign of pleasure—a simple display of joy, of happiness. Smiles connect us. Bind us together. Offer a sense of nearness.

Those of us who walk closely with the Lord are aware of His supernatural smiles in our lives. Every day, in thousands of ways, He sends them our way. His joy abounds when He sees us loving each other. We find God's smiles in a beautiful sunset or the dimples in a child's cheeks. We sense them in the dewy morning, hear them sung in songs of praise on Sunday mornings. We witness them when someone extends a hand of blessing or forgiveness. In short, we're surrounded by the miraculous. The divine.

Oftentimes, though, we miss God's attempts to connect with us. We overlook His love gifts. We're simply not paying attention. Life's busyness has us distracted. Oh, but those heavenly smiles are there! Look around you. See beyond life's painful circumstances. Can you sense God's tenderness toward you? He is pouring out His love, even now.

The stories in this book are filled with God's unending, joyful smiles. May they serve as a reminder of the Lord's ongoing affection toward you. His love never fails, even on the darkest of days. So, lift your heads! Throw wide those arms and prepare yourself for a heavenly embrace as never before. And may you never forget the Father's smiles are meant to be shared with those around you.

For no matter how many promises God has made, they are "Yes" in Christ. And so through him the "Amen" is spoken by us to the glory of God.

2 CORINTHIANS 1:20 NIV

The Blessing

Paula Sjan

Justice Boyson looked from the puppy on the examining table to the smiling vet tech who was checking the pet's heart rate.

"She's a beauty. About twelve weeks old, give or take." She transferred the notes from a clipboard to the computer database. Justice watched her long, tapered fingers fly across the computer keys. He noticed the way her glossy red hair swayed with every movement of her head. She was wearing a paw print-patterned scrub shirt and an oversize dog tag on her lapel with the name "Melody" in cursive script.

"What's her name?"

"Harmony," he answered without thinking. The vet tech gave him an attractive smile, and he detected a look of something—was it amusement?—beneath it.

"That's pretty." She turned back to the keyboard, and Justice shook his head to clear it. He had been considering two names for the dog—Sheba and Roxanne. Where had "Harmony" come from? His subconscious? That's what his mother would say.

"The doctor will be in shortly." As she exited through the door that separated the examining room from the surgery, he felt a rush of warm air and heard the yipping of dogs and the soft brush of rubber-soled shoes on the tile floor, and a stocky, short man entered the room. They shook hands.

"I'm Doctor Fecik."

"Justice."

"Nice to meet you, Justice." The veterinarian lifted the puppy from the stainless steel table and rubbed her throat gently, whispering endearments into her fuzzy, floppy ears. "Good puppy. Good girl," he murmured, as he gently pulled open her mouth and probed her gums. He ran expert hands over her body. She wriggled and tried to climb into the sleeve of his lab coat. "Looks good. A little on the thin side, but solid as a rock. She'll need her puppy shots and a heartworm test today, and we'll schedule a follow-up visit. Where'd you get her?"

"My porch. She just showed up last week. I posted flyers and put an ad in the paper, but no one came. Any idea what kind of dog she is?"

Dr. Fecik smiled. "A lucky one, by the sounds of it." He looked at the computer screen. "Harmony?"

There was something in the doctor's tone that made his words seem more than just a polite inquiry about a dog's name. Justice felt himself blushing. "It just—came to me—like—like the puppy, I guess."

"Fourth Harmony we've had this year. Last year it was eight. Two dogs, six cats." He winked at Justice and smiled broadly. "One was a tom."

"Word association?"

"That's what I figure." Dr. Fecik broke out in merry laughter, and Justice couldn't help but join in.

"She's a mixed breed. Definitely a little spaniel in there, and maybe a terrier of some kind. She's feisty." He retrieved the cord of his stethoscope from between the dog's tiny, sharp teeth and gave her a biscuit from the jar on the counter. "I'll get her started, and meanwhile Melody can get you set up with everything you need."

"That'd be great!" said Justice. He felt the blush rising again. "I mean," he amended, "I could. . .sure use the help."

Melody showed him around the retail area of Pet Pavilion and pointed out the "bare necessities" for owning a puppy. A tiny leather collar that cost more than his newest necktie, a matching leash as supple and shiny as butter, and two miniature stainless steel bowls in a skid-proof rack. He balked at the pink sweater with a bone appliqué she suggested and chose a petite Ohio State Buckeyes T-shirt.

"Do you ever take care of sheep here?" Justice asked, as Melody began scanning items and packing them into brown monogrammed bags.

"No, we're small animals only, but there's a great large-animal vet in Port Clinton. Why? Do you run livestock?" She looked interested.

"No." Justice grinned ruefully. "I feel like I've just been fleeced."

Melody laughed and ran his credit card and gave him a receipt to sign. "You have any other dogs at home?"

"No, this is my first dog. My first pet of any kind. My mother didn't like animals."

"That's too bad."

"Yeah. I always did, though."

"Liked animals?"

"Yeah. Don't know anything about them." He realized that he was still smiling. It had been a long time since he had smiled that much.

"Well if you need anything, you've got my—" He noticed that her cheeks were glowing pink as well. "I mean, the clinic's number's on your receipt."

"That's great," he squeaked. He felt himself blushing again and tried lowering his voice. "I mean. . .great for. . . you know. . .for Harmony."

Melody leaned forward over the counter and spoke softly. "The answer is yes."

"Yes? Yes what?" Now he was really perplexed.

"Yes. I'll go out with you. Tonight. At 7:00. I like comedies, and I insist upon buying the popcorn." She continued to look at him with a Cheshire cat grin and dancing bright green eyes. Finally, Justice found his voice.

"Sure—I mean—um—thank you." He realized he was stammering. He didn't often stammer.

"For what?"

He took in a deep breath and let it out slowly, never taking his gaze from her face. "For saying yes." He searched for something else to say and finally hit upon what he supposed was the right thing. "How about dinner first?" He quickly thought about the receipt he had just buttoned into his shirt pocket and added, "A burger or something."

"Sure. Just let me check real quick." She called over her shoulder, "Dad?" Dr. Fecik came through from the examining room with Harmony under one arm and a squirming gray cat under the other.

"Justice has kindly asked me out for a burger and a movie. Mind feeding the kids tonight?"

Justice's heart sank. *Kids?* he thought. *She's got kids?*

Dr. Fecik smiled affably. "A pleasure." He looked at the mountain of bags on the counter and in the cart. "I see she's found a new retail victim. She didn't talk you into anything you didn't need, did she?"

Justice nodded glumly. He was such a dupe. "Probably. But I managed to dodge a few bullets, too."

"The pink sweater with the bone?" Justice nodded. "She's been trying to foist that monstrosity onto unsuspecting fellows for a month." Dr. Fecik fixed Melody with a mock stern look and tried to draw himself up to appear taller, but his daughter towered above him. She kissed him on the top of his half-bald head.

"Diversification, Daddy. It's the name of the game now for small business, and you know our profits have gone up 30 percent since we added the pretty pooch line."

"True." He deposited Harmony in the shopping basket where she curled into a ball of fluff atop the new faux-fleece crate liner and promptly fell asleep. The vet crooned to the cat as he carried it back to surgery.

Justice thought, *I might as well bite the bullet now.* To Melody he said, "You've got kids? How many?" He tried to sound casual, but his voice betrayed him with another squeak.

"Nine—no, ten, I guess. Dad's always bringing home strays. That gray tom you just saw? That's number ten. He was abandoned by the old railroad depot on Saturday."

Justice was so relieved he almost shouted. "Oh! Ten pets—ten—animals! I thought—" He cut himself off, but not before she grasped his meaning. Once again she laughed with contagious merriment.

Melody met him at the Burgers 'n' Things that night, and several other nights that week. She was a wonderful companion. They began to meet earlier so they could linger over their burgers or tacos and talk. By the second week they didn't bother with a movie. They just ate and talked, sitting in the window booth at Burgers 'n' Things or under the willow tree at Petermund Park. Sometimes they met on the porch of the Fecik home, where Dr. Fecik could join them and contribute to the conversation.

They talked about their mothers, and the cancer that had taken them both. They talked about animal care and Melody's scholarship to vet school at Cornell University. She was thrilled with the opportunity—and sorry it would be so far away. She was best friends with her father; Justice's greatest sadness was never having known his. She liked chocolate. He liked vanilla. They spoke of inconsequential trivia and weighty matters with equal ease. This kind of discourse was new for him. He discovered that he had opinions about such diverse subjects as politics, soybeans, and non-chlorine bleach, and no opinion at all about glee clubs, telephone conglomerates, or beet sugar. He wondered how they found so many things to talk about. His own home had been a place of silence and stillness long before his mother had become ill.

There had been few books in the home of his youth, and there were fewer still in his apartment over the store. A yellow phone book dotted with on-hold graffiti, the newest copy of Sports Illustrated, a mint-condition leather-bound Bible from his baptism twenty-six years ago, a few how-to books, and the various trade catalogs with which his mailbox was always glutted.

The Fecik home was crammed with reading material. Built-in floor-to-ceiling bookshelves lined the long living room. Books and journals covered every hard surface in the den. Even the bright yellow kitchen boasted a rack of neatly arranged cookbooks on top of the refrigerator.

"Melody," he asked one evening as she washed their drinking glasses and he folded away the Chinese take-out cartons and placed them in the dog-proof garbage pail, "may I borrow one of your books?"

"Of course. Take your pick."

He lifted down a large tome with a dusty red cover. "This one."

She looked at the book and nodded. "That's a good one. Belonged to my mom. She always made the Hawaiian pie." Melody sounded a little wistful when she spoke. She touched the book gently. "See that?" She opened the book and pointed to a grubby brown mark on the flyleaf. "That's her thumbprint. She put it there the day she got the book. Just dipped her thumb in chocolate syrup and printed it." She smiled, and tears welled up in her eyes.

"Why?"

"So she could enjoy the book without worrying about getting the first mark on it."

"Oh." Justice thought he understood. It was like the first ding on a new car. It was inevitable, and one could spend an inordinate amount of time thinking of ways to avoid it, all to no avail. He looked at her warmly and whispered in her ear, "The answer is yes."

With an anticipatory smile she said, "Yes, what?"

"Yes, I will make you the Hawaiian pie."

She laughed and more tears sprang to her eyes. Then, before he knew what was happening, she leaned against his chest. He instinctively wrapped his arms around her and held her as she cried. He wept, too. For Melody. For her mother. For the mother that he would never see again. For every time he had been afraid to let a tear fall, he wept. This, too, was inevitable. Why had he spent so much time keeping grief at arm's length? Long minutes passed, and when the sobs had quieted into sniffs, he found the words of the pastor at the funeral coming back to him. "To be absent from the body is to be present with Christ. . . ." He tried to think of the rest.

"To be absent from the body—" he fell silent, as he realized that he had spoken aloud.

"Is to be present with Christ." The words came from the yielding form in his arms. He gently stepped back from her and looked into her now-red and streaming eyes.

"Do you believe that?" he asked.

She nodded. "More than anything. Do you?" She waited, unblinking, as Justice searched for the truth. Finally, he nodded.

"Yes, I do. I had forgotten that I believe that, but I do."

"I'm so happy you remembered," she murmured as she pressed her wet face against his shoulder. He felt a lump rise in his throat and his voice was unsteady as he answered.

"Me, too." Justice heard a rustling in the hallway, but when he turned around he saw only Harmony, intent upon the destruction of a leather house shoe.

The next few months sped by. Justice was happier than he ever remembered being. Since the death of his mother three years before, he had been constantly aware of a feeling of heaviness, of loneliness. As manager of the Main Street Hardware Store, he was surrounded by people all day: handymen looking for plumbing supplies, farmers buying gardening implements and barn paint, and young people from the community college dropping in to sign out the lend-a-hammer. And yet the loneliness had lingered—until now.

It was Saturday night. Dr. Fecik had made them a fine spaghetti dinner with crispy garlic rolls and a crunchy green salad harvested that day from Melody's carefully tended garden. They had ended the meal with a perfectly presented Hawaiian pie loaded with fresh pineapple and bananas and topped with coconut cream. How wonderful it felt to sit on the Feciks' stoop in the long shadows of a summer evening, with Melody by his side and the almost full-grown Harmony at his feet. Dr. Fecik sat on the glider, surrounded by dogs and cats.

For a long time no one felt a need to speak. It was enough to sit in peaceful proximity to one another. The night sounds began. Crickets warmed up their chirping, mosquitoes buzzed, the well pump hummed, the glider clicked respectfully under its burden as the vet slowly rocked. It was Dr. Fecik who broke the silence.

"The answer is yes."

All eyes were fixed on him. The dogs watched him carefully, waiting for the word treat to signal their bedtime snack. The cats stretched their slender necks inquiringly, wondering if the vet was finally going to remove himself from their glider. Justice and Melody looked at him with amusement, waiting for the punch line. There were rules to this game, and it hadn't taken Justice long to figure them out.

"Yes, what?" he asked, grinning at the vet.

"Yes, you may marry my daughter." Justice's jaw dropped open. "Don't gape at me. I'm sure she'd get around to asking you eventually, but she's going to school in August, and I can't take the suspense all the way to Christmas break."

Dr. Fecik stood up abruptly, and various animals tumbled from his lap. He gave his daughter a warm look and then met Justice's eyes. "To be absent from the body is indeed to be present with Christ. Thank you for reminding me." He hugged his daughter and turned to lay a strong, warm hand on Justice's shoulder. "Good night, son. Receive a father's blessing."

I will praise the Lord at all times.

I will constantly speak his praises.

PSALM 34:1 NLT

Two Strong Legs

SHERRY'S STORY (AS TOLD TO AMY BLAKE)

I helped my three-year-old son into the car, set my Bible on the seat, and closed the door. Shading my eyes with one hand, I watched my husband hoe our garden. His strong body battled the weeds crowding our plants, and his determined face made it clear he would win the fight.

I steeled myself and called, "Terry, we're heading for church now."

He stopped work and stomped across the grass toward me. I cringed, seeing in his face the anger only my newfound faith provoked.

Before he could start hollering, I worked up enough nerve to ask, "Do you want to go with us this time?"

His face reddened, and he ripped off his work gloves. "How many times do I have to tell you, Sherry? I don't need your religious crutch!"

I bit my lip. In the car beside me, Shawn began to whimper.

Heedless, Terry slammed a glove to the ground and pointed at our house. "Who bought you this house?"

"You did," I whispered.

He flung the other glove down next to the car where our son now sobbed, frightened by his daddy's rage. "Who bought you this car?"

"You did," I whispered again, fighting my own tears.

"That's right, me! Not your God!" He smacked his hands against his thighs. "As long as I have this healthy body and these two strong legs, I'll never need your God!"

He glared at me, snatched up his gloves, and stalked back to the garden plot.

Trembling, I walked around the car, climbed inside, and tried to soothe my son. "Hush, Shawn-baby, it'll be okay; you'll see. Mama loves you."

I covered my face, leaned my forehead against the steering wheel, and begged God to save my husband's soul.

The next night, I stared at the sputtering candles as the special dinner I'd prepared grew cold. I'd found out just that day I was two months pregnant with our second child, and I couldn't wait to tell Terry he was going to be a daddy again.

But my husband was late. Very late.

Finally, the ringing phone shattered the silence. Terry had been in a car accident.

Thankful Shawn was at the neighbor's house, I rushed to the hospital, only to learn that my husband was in surgery. He wasn't expected to live through the night. Thinking of our two little ones, I pleaded with God to spare their daddy.

While I waited for word, I decided I should check

on the people who'd been in the other car. With Terry so terribly injured, I knew the other driver must be bad off.

But when I asked the receptionist if I could visit him and his family, she avoided my eyes. "They released him."

I blinked. "Already? Wasn't he hurt?"

She shook her head, still not meeting my eyes.

"Well," I said quietly, "his wife must be so grateful."

She nodded with her lips clamped shut. After a second, she grabbed my hand. "Listen, honey, it's only right for you to know. . . . The other driver was drunk as a skunk. He was driving without a license on the wrong side of the road." She squeezed my fingers until they stung. "It's all his fault, and he didn't get so much as a scratch."

She watched me, probably expecting me to throw a fit. I simply nodded and walked away, feeling numb, like I'd been punched until I couldn't feel the punches anymore.

When I got back to the waiting room, I sat in a quiet corner. I told myself that I should be furious, that the drunken fool deserved to be dying in surgery instead of my husband, that no one would blame me for hating him.

But God protected my heart. I focused my remaining energy on praying for Terry's survival.

In the morning, the doctor came. "Ma'am, your husband survived the night, and we think he'll live."

I burst into tears, and he patted my shoulder.

"I have to warn you, though—" His weary eyes

radiated compassion. "Your husband will never walk again. His legs were mangled in the accident, and his feet were crushed. It'll be a long time before he recovers enough even to go home."

Over the next weeks, life delivered one blow after another to my young faith. Only now I wasn't numb to them. My soul felt each and every agonizing jab.

Four days after the accident, I sat down at the kitchen table with our insurance papers and sighed, thankful that at least we had good health coverage.

When I called the company to report Terry's accident and arrange payment for his hospital bills, the representative grew quiet. After a moment, he said, "Ma'am, I'm afraid I have bad news about your account."

I braced my hands against the smooth wooden tabletop. *God, please. . .* "What do you mean?"

"Our agent came to your house each month for cash payments, is that correct?"

I swallowed hard. "Yes, he told us the rates were better that way."

Silence. Then, "I hate to tell you this, but he was pocketing the cash you gave him. He disappeared two days ago. The police are looking for him." Another silence. "I'm sorry, ma'am, your husband has no coverage with our company. Perhaps he has a policy through his place of employment?"

I hung up without answering. His place of

employment? There was no employment now, and I'd stopped working three years before when Shawn was born.

I ran out to the garden and knelt in the dirt. I cradled my hands over the unborn child growing in my womb and wept. *God, are You there? Do You see?*

When I finally cried myself dry, I straightened my spine and started pulling weeds. More than ever, we needed whatever produce I could preserve from this little garden.

Over the next weeks, I developed a routine. I'd spend each long day sitting at my husband's bedside, trying to hide the way my heart hurt as I watched his once-strong body now crushed and wracked with pain, wasting away in that white hospital bed.

Each evening, I'd return to the loneliness of an empty house because I'd sent Shawn to stay at my parents' home more than an hour away. Each night, I'd phone my little boy and listen as he begged to come home to me and his daddy. And each time I'd tell him the same thing: "Hush, Shawn-baby, it'll be okay; you'll see. Mama loves you. We'll all be together again soon."

I'd hang up with my little boy's homesick cries still echoing in my heart and run out to the garden, my one place of solace, to tend the plants we so desperately needed. *Is it true, God? Is it going to be okay? Will we be together again soon?*

Then one night a terrible storm swept through. It

pounded our poor garden until nothing was left. I was too depressed even to weep. My beaten soul was as barren and hopeless as the little plot Terry and I had worked so hard to make productive. Would we survive?

Seven months after the accident, an ambulance brought Terry home. A body cast covered him from armpits to toes. That night, I gave birth to our second son, Barry.

During the next months, my battered faith was tested beyond all I could imagine. I alone had responsibility for a newborn, a three-year-old, and an atheist in a body cast. Since we owned our home, we didn't qualify for government assistance. My folks gave us what they could, but still I had to juggle bills.

One icy day, I received a shut-off notice from the electric company. I'd heard the government was offering to pay the electric bill for people who needed help if we went to their office, so I bundled up the boys and we went to stand in the long line. An elderly lady in line behind me kept doubling over coughing. She swayed on her feet, and I thought she was going to faint. She told me she was sick, but that she needed this help to keep the heat on.

Finally, when I was next up to enter the office, the lady had a particularly bad coughing fit. My heart tugged. I told her, "You can go ahead of us."

She thanked me and went. When she came out, the government worker came out with her and said, "We're out of funds, folks. I'm sorry."

Feeling like I'd been slapped, I took Shawn's small hand, cradled Barry close, and walked home. *God? This is what I get for trying to show kindness? Don't You care?*

Later that week, after I'd spent our last penny to pay the electric bill, I sat at the kitchen table staring at the empty cabinets. My family needed to eat, and I had no way to feed them. But studying God's Word had taught me He was in charge of all things, so I cried out to Him for help. *You promised to meet our needs, God.*

I prayed a long time until I felt compelled to check my coat pockets. I found twenty dollars. My weary heart filled with praise, and I hurried to the local IGA to buy formula for my baby and food for my husband and son.

I picked up a pound of hamburger, thinking of the chili I planned to make, when the grocer took the meat from my hands. He wrote a much lower price on the package and handed it back to me.

"Thank you," I said and put it in my cart.

The man smiled and picked up another package. He marked it down and handed it to me. Then he did the same with another. And another. And another.

He looked at me. "I have no idea why I just did that."

I smiled. "That's okay. I do." *God, You're amazing.*

—

On Easter Sunday morning, my baby toddled around my husband's wheelchair. Terry had graduated from the body cast to leg casts. Still the doctor said he'd never walk.

I was almost ready for church by the time I worked up the courage to ask, "Terry, would you attend Easter services with us?"

He shocked me by saying yes. *Thank You, God.*

We sat in the back of the crowded sanctuary. Terry's wheelchair was parked in the aisle beside my seat. He held one son on his lap while I held the other. The church choir sang "One Day Too Late," a song about an unbelieving husband's grief when his wife and children go to heaven without him. Tears streamed down Terry's face.

After church, he took my hand and said, "That's me, Sherry. You're going to heaven without me because I refused to believe in God." He gestured toward our boys playing on the floor, their bellies full from lunch. "I know now that God's the One who provided all this, not me." He patted his legs—legs that had been casted for nearly two years. "Because I can't."

"But it's not too late for you," I told him. "God spared your life so you could learn that He's God. That He's in control of the universe instead of you."

"But how can He forgive me for what I said? The way I acted?"

So I shared the Gospel with my husband that day, and Jesus saved his soul.

Now, thirty-five years later, I climb into the passenger side of the car and smile as my husband closes the door for me. He hobbles around to the driver's side, clutching a cane with one hand and a Bible with the other. He'll never walk without pain, but against the doctor's predictions, he *is* walking. His face shines with a peace and joy that wasn't there before the "accident."

And me? I praise the God of grace every day for being my husband's two strong legs.

"Give, and it will be given to you. A good measure, pressed down, shaken together and running over, will be poured into your lap. For with the measure you use, it will be measured to you."

LUKE 6:38 NIV

The Angel of Bosnia

David McLaughlan

When I set out with the children that day I wasn't looking for angels.

We were on holiday in the north of England and staying by a particularly impressive stretch of coast. When the tide was out, you could see a series of giant circular patterns in the rock. I'm sure there is a geological explanation for them but, as far as the kids and I were concerned, as we looked down from the cliff top, it looked like God Himself had stuck His finger in the molten rock and swirled it around.

The previous year, when I had last been in the area, I had found an interesting but old and abandoned structure near the edge of the cliffs. Two stories high, it was a tall concrete box with big, unglazed windows looking out to the sea. The remains of a balcony ran around three of the walls.

I had thought eleven-year-old Amy and ten-year-old Josh might like to explore it, (carefully, of course). But when we got there things had changed dramatically. The balcony had been rebuilt, the windows were glazed, there was a flag flying from the roof, and there was a man up there peering out to sea through a pair of binoculars.

Coming closer we saw a table arranged outside the building. Secondhand books and homemade bookmarks were for sale—a fundraiser for a group called Sea-watch. There was also a laminated invitation to climb the ladder by the side wall and visit.

"Do you want to?" I challenged the kids.

"Do *you* want to?" they replied, nervously.

"Come on." I laughed. "Let's go!"

The Sea-watch guys were great. They made the children feel welcome, and they were only too happy to answer my questions.

The tower had been built during WWII. Looking out across the North Sea it was manned by the Home Guard in an attempt to spot any possible enemy incursions. Thankfully, none came that way, and it was soon abandoned. The Coast Guard used it for a while. Now this voluntary group occupied it. They were a reference point and information station for tourists. They handed out sunscreen and warned about tides and dangerous currents. They looked out for boats in trouble and passed information to the police about the occasional smuggling that went on in the area.

As a way to spend some of your retirement years, I thought, *I have seen a lot worse.*

One of the guys, though, seemed a little different from the rest. His military background was given away by his bearing—oh, and the fact that the other men referred to him as "the Major."

At the time I was writing articles for magazines and was always on the lookout for a good story. After hearing a thing or two that piqued my interest, I asked if I might be able to come back sometime and interview him. He agreed, but the children weren't so obliging.

"Why not do it now?" Amy asked.

The Major laughed and shrugged. The sea was quiet, and he did like to tell his story! Josh and Amy climbed onto the swivel chairs by the window, and, recognizing I was outnumbered, I gave in gracefully. I took out my notepad and began scribbling like mad to keep up with the Major's tale of wonder.

Service was deeply rooted in this man. After a career as "something in the military" and a short stint in the priesthood, he had retired to the northeast coast, but not to sit with his feet up. So, after discovering the abandoned watchtower, he rustled up some like-minded souls, found funding, and set up Sea-watch.

Having escaped Saigon just before the fall (by paying "thousands" to get out of the country), the Major and his wife arrived in England with just over fifteen dollars between them. Needing a change of direction, and wanting to get away from the military, he headed for the priesthood.

At around the same time Czechoslovakia fell apart and the Bosnian war broke out, the Major was conducting a service at Oxford University chapel with a colleague who would later go on to become the Queen's chaplain.

"There was a girl crying her eyes out in the church," he told us. "Her father was a Serbian and her mother a Croat, and she said to me, 'Would you help us?'

"I said, 'Yes.' And she said, 'In front of Jesus, swear an oath!' So, I did.

"My colleague offered to take the service, and I turned away to make us some coffee. When I turned back, she was gone. My colleague said she hadn't left past him. But there wasn't another way out. Not usually a man to comment on such things, he just couldn't get over how beautiful she had been. When I told him about the oath, I'd been surprised to find I had just made, he said, 'Well. . .you better do something about it then, hadn't you.'

"So, I went on TV and said we'd be sending two truckloads of aid to Bosnia. I didn't know how to get permits. I didn't know how to get trucks. I had no idea how to get supplies! But in fourteen days we had twenty-one tons of aid ready to go. We had five drivers. They got shot up a bit. . ."

The memory of these attacks on people only trying to help sobered him for a moment.

"Then I got a call from the Croatian Embassy, which then consisted of one room. They needed supplies for a maternity hospital. It just so happened I had a visitor in the church at that very moment who knew who to ask. I rang them, and within twenty-four hours they got thousands of those specific supplies from Edinburgh to us in Cambridge. They were then flown out to Zagreb and were being used within forty-eight hours of that request being made.

"We had a call from the Shetland Isles, offering forty tons of educational materials. How were we going to get it from the Shetlands, far off the north coast of Scotland, to Oxford in the south of England? Well, amazingly, the German navy brought it down to us for free!

"Things just seemed to happen like that! Funny things happened as well. A chap rang up asking if we would like some gripe water used to settle babies' stomachs. We thought it might be a box of bottles. He sent us ninety-six thousand bottles of the stuff. There were a lot of burping babies in those Bosnian, Slovenian, and Croatian hospitals when that delivery arrived!

"In two years we shipped a thousand tons. In five years, another six thousand. By now my career in the church had taken a distant second place to helping the Bosnian people."

I commented on how inspirational the people he worked with must have been and could only wonder how this must have contrasted with the horrors other men perpetrated.

"Yup! I visited one camp of seven hundred women whose husbands had all been murdered. We're only on this earth a short time. Why can't we just get along?"

When the Major closed his operation down, he had letters of thanks from thirteen ambassadors and two heads of state. But this was dismissed with a wave of the hand. For the Major it was all about the people.

"Oh, we'll never be rich," he said, "but I've helped people, and I can live with that."

By the end of the operation, his doctor suggested his health had suffered.

"Well," he explained, "we were always getting calls in the middle of the night, and I could never say no. You would get the ambassador of one country saying, 'We need a planeload for a hospital,' or someone else would need help in another country. It got so I couldn't sleep and my nerves were shattered."

Taking a shipment of aid to a port on the English Channel for shipping to Europe and knowing the lifetime organization of a hardy band of volunteers was coming to an end, he spotted a group doing voluntary work along that stretch of coast and decided he could do something similar in the northeast. And so, Sea-watch came into being.

At the first meeting, he had four volunteers turn up. The police and local authority told him he was wasting his time. "But that kind of response only makes me more determined.

"The first winter we had no doors and no windows.

We all got the flu. But the word spread, and it really took off."

He regaled us with some of the things that had happened over the years. He'd pulled someone's sinking car from the sands using his own car as a tow truck. The fellow had said, "Thank you very much," and drove off. The Major had to pay fifteen hundred pounds to get his own car repaired afterward. They made welcome a group of four hundred city kids who had never been to the seaside before. He had taken a group of visitors on a moonlit night hike along the cliff tops when they heard some desperate voices. Two elderly ladies, stopping for the night on their way to London, had decided to take their dogs for an evening stroll on the sands. They had been cut off. Backed against the cliffs by the rising tide, they had no option but to scream for help and hope someone heard.

Those ladies, like so many other people, had cause to be glad that the Major was around.

Well, the story seemed to be coming to an end. My hand was cramping from taking notes. The children had sat, engrossed, through most of it, but now those swivel chairs were swiveling more and more toward the spectacular view out the windows.

We talked a little about his plans to expand Sea-watch into other coastal areas. I told him how impressed I was with all his work and thanked him for his time.

Like a gentleman, he climbed down the ladder first,

just in case the children slipped. I put a contribution in the collection tin and shook his hand warmly. It had been a genuine pleasure to meet this extraordinary man.

As I was about to turn away and walk back to the hotel, I remembered the girl in the church, that extraordinarily beautiful young woman who belonged to both sides of a war. Since the Major kept his promise to her, everything seemed to have fallen into place. Her tears had generated a major humanitarian movement. An obvious idea occurred to me, but I hesitated to put it into words.

Seeing my consternation the Major asked, "Was there something else?"

I put my embarrassment aside and asked, "Do you think she could have been an angel? That girl in the church."

It obviously wasn't the first time the idea had crossed his mind, but he stuck his jaw out defiantly. "I don't believe in that sort of thing anymore," he said flatly. "I find it hard to see God in some of the things I've seen."

I was temporarily at a loss for something to say. Then my daughter filled the gap. I don't know if this was something she had heard in Sunday school or something that had just occurred to her, but it was the perfect thing to say.

"Maybe if you didn't see God it was because He was behind you, pushing you in the right direction."

The silence that followed was broken only by the

wind and the seagulls. Then the Major smiled at my daughter.

"The older I get," he said slowly, "the more I think that just might be true."

It was a moment that could only be described as "hopeful" all around.

The fear of the LORD is the beginning of wisdom,

and knowledge of the Holy One is understanding.

For through wisdom your days will be many,

and years will be added to your life.

PROVERBS 9:10—11 NIV

Swing Away

MARTHA WILLEY

I could hardly contain my excitement as we pulled into my sister's driveway.

"Tell me again what Aunt Susan said to you when she called this morning," my daughter Carol asked as she turned off the car engine.

"She told me she had a time machine and that I should come right over and see it," I said.

"Oh," Carol said thoughtfully.

"I know your aunt can seem a bit strange now and then, but she sounded just fine this morning."

"You don't think talking about a time machine is strange, Mother?"

Actually I had found it a bit odd, even for Susan. My sister had slowly been developing holes in her thinking, but I wasn't as bothered by these lapses of time or the crazy notions Susan came up with as the rest of my family was. I would just respond to whatever place and time Susan thought she was in.

My daughter wouldn't have known anything about Susan's claim of a time machine had I not needed her to drive me to Susan's house. Carol, along with my son Chet, sat me down a week ago and told me the time had come to hand over my car keys. "You're almost eighty-five Mother, and with the recent accidents you've had we feel it's time for you to stop driving and let us take you where you need to go," Carol said.

I objected of course. "All I hit was the mailbox."

"And the neighbor's car," Carol said.

"You ran into your own garage, Mother," Chet said.

I could not convince them otherwise, so now I was at the mercy of their schedule and their comments about visiting my sister who was slowly slipping away into a world of her own making.

Carol's next comment brought my thoughts back to the time at hand. "I just know that when I talked to Becky yesterday she said her mother was having a bad day. Aunt Susan stood at the front door all day waiting for Uncle Romer to come home from work. How could she forget that her own husband died ten years ago? Becky was beside herself."

"Becky's always beside herself." I loved Susan's daughter, Becky, but she could be a bit high-strung. "Becky needs to do what God says—worry less, trust more."

"I just don't want you getting upset if Aunt Susan isn't herself today," Carol said.

"I'm not an easily crushed flower, Carol," I snapped. When I saw her hurt expression, I felt a stab of regret. "God will give me the strength to face whatever mood Susan's in. I'll be fine honey, really. Now please help me out of the car."

In a few minutes my niece Becky was letting us into the farmhouse she and my sister share.

"Mother's out back with her time machine," Becky said smiling.

"Not you, too." Carol groaned shaking her head.

"Come on, Aunt June. I'll help you out to the backyard," Becky offered.

"I can find my own way," I said, pushing my walker along in front of me. I came to the back door of the house and looked out. There sat my older sister Susan on a porch swing. I couldn't believe that with her bad hip she was able to swing.

She greeted me with a huge smile. "Oh June, you're here. Isn't this just wonderful? Becky bought it for me as an early birthday present."

The swing was made out of white wicker. The thick seat cushions were covered with a bird-print material that was soft to the touch and beautiful.

"Sit down and take a load off," Susan said with a smile.

I eased my body down. My behind had barely touched the cushion when she pushed us off. "Isn't this grand?" she asked.

I looked at where the swing was attached to the ceiling. "Are you sure this thing is safe?"

"Very. My son-in-law super-reinforced it. Stop worrying. Isn't this fun?"

A soft breeze caressed my face. My niece's flowerbeds were an array of colors—red, orange, yellow, and white. Yellow finches fed at one of the many birdfeeders in the yard. A wind chime gently jingled nearby. I felt myself relaxing. "You know, I can't remember the last time I sat on a swing," I said.

"This isn't a swing. . .it's a time machine," Susan said.

I looked at my sister, and tears stung my eyes. I resolved to stay strong. I played along. "And where are we going to be traveling to?" I asked.

Susan laughed. "I've got both oars in the water, June, at least at this moment. I know we're sitting in a swing. But it's also a time machine."

"What do you mean?"

"Do you remember our old swing set? How the ropes cut into our hands?"

My mind cycled back through the years, and soon the memory of my swing set became clear. The seats were wooden boards painted red, and the metal poles were bright blue. How I loved swinging, pumping my legs as fast as I could, my ponytail bouncing back and forth in the breeze.

"Yes, I remember. I haven't thought about that swing set in years."

Susan smiled. "We used to get so high up in those swings that we could see all the way to the Nichols' dairy farm over a block away."

"Mom caught us one time, remember? She came running out of the house and yelled at us to never swing that high again."

"She was always afraid the ropes would break and we'd go sailing off into space," Susan said. "Did I ever tell you I once caught Mom outside on my swing?"

I looked at my sister, shocked. "No. Really? Mom was swinging?" I just couldn't imagine my mother sitting on a swing. She would always push us, but she refused to swing herself.

"She was up every bit as high as we used to go."

I smiled at the image of my prim and proper mother swinging. "What did she say?"

"She said only adults were allowed that high, not twelve-year-old girls."

"Just wait until I join her in heaven one day. I'm going to remind her of her double standard." I laughed.

We lapsed into silence for a few minutes, just enjoying the whooshing sound of the swing going back and forth.

"Do you remember any of the things we talked about while we were swinging?" Susan asked.

I chuckled. "Do you know how many years back you're asking me to go?"

"Come on. One memory."

"Well, okay. We used to talk about what we were going to be when we grew up. You were going to be a famous painter with your artwork hung up in museums all over the world."

"You were going to be a princess and a librarian." Susan giggled.

"I got one out of the two. Do you regret that you never got to go to art school?"

Susan married right out of high school because her boyfriend was being sent to France to fight in the war. She found work in a factory; then when he returned they started raising their family. The only time she picked up a paintbrush after that was when she was painting her children's bedrooms.

"Now and then, but God helped me make peace with that a long time ago. Besides, can you imagine me in college? You know what kind of student I was."

"The one voted most likely to think of trouble, cause trouble, and be in trouble."

"You weren't always an angel yourself," she reminded me as she gave the swing a push.

"True," I admitted. "I wonder what ever became of Mr. Stillman."

"The teacher who looked like Cary Grant?"

"I was *so* in love with him," I swooned. I felt my face grow red as Susan stared at me.

"I didn't know that. You never told me."

"You would have laughed."

"Probably. But I wouldn't have laughed for very long.

You know, I saw him the other day at the pharmacy. He said he has to take about a dozen pills to keep his body going."

"I suppose he's fat and flabby."

"Who?"

"Mr. Stillman."

"Were we talking about him?" Susan asked as the swing slowed down.

"Yes." I gave the swing another push.

"Just now? I. . .ah. . .don't remember." She looked so troubled I reached over and patted her hand. "I hate it when my mind fails me." Tears sparkled in her eyes.

"It's okay, dear." I handed her a tissue from my purse. "Let's switch to someone more interesting. Billy Harsher." I hoped Susan would remember him. All the girls at our school had a crush on Billy Harsher. He was like a Ken doll, perfect in every way and always with a smile on his face.

Susan beamed. "Who could forget him? Remember how we used to sit on our swings and call ourselves Mrs. Billy Harsher?"

I nodded. "When we were swinging we never had to worry about Mom and Dad overhearing us talking about the cute boys at school."

"They would have had a fit if they knew how boy crazy we were." Susan laughed.

"Remember the time you jumped out of the swing

and broke your foot?"

"That was bad." Susan nodded.

"Bad? You got to lie around eating ice cream while I had to do all your chores."

"Yes, but I couldn't swing. I felt like I was a bird whose wings had been clipped."

She still sounded sad over missing time out on her swing.

I gave her arm a squeeze. "What else do you remember?"

"The concerts we gave."

I burst out laughing. We used to sing hymns at the top of our lungs while we swung. "It's a wonder no one ever called the cops on us for disturbing the peace."

"Remember the time we tried to paint our fingernails while we were swinging?"

"Or that time the fly flew in your mouth?"

We went back and forth reminding each other of all the conversations that took place while we were swinging. After a while we turned from the past to the present. I told her how much I hated not having my car.

Susan told me that Becky was going to quit her job because she didn't want Susan home by herself. "She says she doesn't mind, that this gives her a chance to do for me after all the years I used to do for her."

"Carol's said the same thing to me. It's still strange, though, don't you think? To have our children waiting on us?"

Susan nodded. "When God said He would meet my needs I never thought it would be through my children."

We lapsed into silence then, weighted down by thoughts of our aging and the limitations it put on us.

Suddenly I grabbed Susan's hand. "What is it?" she gasped. "Did you throw your hip out?"

"No. I was just thinking that when Dad put those swings up, we were too little to get them going. We needed him or Mom to give us a push."

"So?"

"If we hadn't let them help us, we would have been stuck. Accepting an offer of an extended hand isn't a bad thing, and you know I don't exactly mind not having to smile for a driver's license photo. I always looked like a hoodlum."

Susan considered this. "Hmm, it *is* kind of nice not having to figure out what to cook for dinner."

"No paying for gas!" I joyously shouted.

"No dusting!" Susan giggled.

"No having to do laundry."

"No Raisin Bran."

I stared at Susan. "What?"

"I get to eat the same marshmallow sweet stuff the grandkids eat."

"With no car insurance to pay for, I can afford to buy material for the quilt I've always said I was going to make."

"And I can get the puppy I never could have when I was living in my apartment."

"Perhaps our current life changes aren't too awful after all," I admitted.

"We've been really blessed when you consider our eighty-some years of life," Susan mused.

"God has faithfully provided for us just like He promised He would."

"Definitely. I may forget Him, but I know He won't forget me," Susan said.

I gave her a quick hug.

Becky stuck her head outside the back door, "If you two 'swingers' are done, lunch is ready."

"Coming," Susan said. We let the swing stop.

"We've had some of our best times on a swing, haven't we?" I said.

"It's where I learned I could come to you about anything."

"It's where I learned you would be there if I needed you," I said. "I never realized how sitting on a swing would bring back so many wonderful memories. You were right to call this a time machine."

Susan smiled. "You know one of the nicest things about a time machine swing is you can get on board for a ride anytime." She and I looked at each other and began pumping our legs as fast as our arthritis would allow.

"I don't think a few more minutes of time travel will hurt," I said, grinning.

Susan smiled. "Swing away, sister, swing away."

Christ is the visible image of the invisible God. He existed before anything was created and is supreme over all creation, for through him God created everything in the heavenly realms and on earth. He made the things we can see and the things we can't see—such as thrones, kingdoms, rulers, and authorities in the unseen world. Everything was created through him and for him. He existed before anything else, and he holds all creation together.

Colossians 1:15-17 nlt

The Sign of the Pink Flamingo

Valorie Quesenberry

Ellen peeked around the corner of the house and
chuckled. It was perfect. And what a beautiful day for her
little scheme—sunny as usual in northern Florida, but one
of those days that had a tang of citrus in the air and a glint
of gold in the sky. Not too hot. Made you glad you had
given the coats to Goodwill, tossed the snow shovel in the
dump, and embraced life in paradise.

Yeah, she had been hesitant when Richie announced
his desire to be a permanent snowbird. But, land's sake,
she wasn't one of those girls who couldn't admit to being
wrong once in a while. And being down here gave them
a good excuse to take a few road trips each year to see the
grandkids. And how she and Rich loved to ramble! My,
they had always been a pair of globe-trotters.

Ellen pulled the steaks out of the fridge and set
about mixing up the marinade. None of those envelope
mixes for her. A little vinegar, some olive oil, a dash of
Worcestershire, and some sprinkles of several different
spices and watch out, Food Channel! Ellen's steaks were
legendary in the family.

Now, back to the musings. . . Oh sure, the trips they
made. Well, back in the day, the Hartons were quite the
family for taking that annual vacation; and after the kids
left home, she and Richie had seen no reason to curtail

their traveling penchant. Oh, the miles they had logged on that old Dodge. In her mind's eye, Ellen could see it now, plowing down the highway, she and Rich with the windows rolled down, a couple cans of soda in the console, and the open road ahead of them.

"That's the way to adventure!" Richie always said of a morning. It was his way of starting the day, telling her that he was ready to hit it hard again.

Putting the steaks in the fridge, Ellen leaned down and lifted the foil on the dessert. Yes, it was setting nicely. Jell-O cake was another of her specialties. She imagined Rich getting ready to enjoy a large slab, slathered in whipped topping. He had a way of smoothing out the whipped cream on top with his fork before he took the first bite. It was a kind of ritual.

Ellen sat down to take a breather. It wasn't all it was cracked up to be, this getting older. She risked a look at her ankles and shook her head. How did they have the nerve to get puffy like that? Ellen Billings Harton had always had the slimmest, most delicate ankles of the bunch. Well, that's what Richie always said. Just like him to say something like that, too. He wasn't like other men, her Rich. He had a knack for noticing the unusual, the small, the ordinary. And she loved him for it.

That's why she was sure she had made a good choice. Oh, that man had better come home on time from his fishing trip today. . . .

"What happens now?"

Noel slapped her palms on the desk and sighed. It was always the same. You get to a point in the story and the ends begin to unravel. How to keep it together? Should it be happy or sad? Tragic or triumphant? Maybe Richie will die on his fishing trip, and Ellen will plant the pink flamingo at his grave as an eclectic reminder of their love. What if Ellen is really a nursing home resident with Alzheimer's disease and this story is taking place in her mind and she dies to be reunited with Richie? Maybe it should be a bland, fluffy story where Richie comes home, Ellen burns the steaks, and they all live happily ever after, chortling about their horrid pink flamingo in the front yard. And why a flamingo anyway? Noel shook her head; she hated those awkward-looking birds. Why had she chosen that as an icon of lasting love?

A drive. . . . She needed to get out of the house. Sure, it was ten below and snowing furiously. That's why she had set the story in Florida. For goodness' sake, a writer did have the luxury of imagination.

Alaska was a land of wonders, to be sure. Every time Noel set her foot outside the door, she wondered how any living creature survived here—darkness for weeks at a time and the bone-gripping cold that clenched this primal, fascinating wilderness.

She unplugged the contraption that kept her car battery from freezing and started the engine. *Thank you, Daddy, for making me buy a good car.*

Backing out of the garage, Noel headed to Walmart. Always open, good American enterprise that they were.

She needed a few things anyway—batteries and maybe some orange juice. All that writing about Florida made something citrus sound good.

The highway department was doing their job. The parking lot was doable. Of course, most of the people who lived here could drive in a blizzard blindfolded. It came with the lifestyle. There was a code of stoutheartedness around here. The people, quite simply, were amazing. And, as yet, Noel hadn't made it into the club.

She was thankful for her boots on the tramp into the store. And, oh, wonderful heat blowers that blasted with gale force as you stepped into the outer entrance. Just like an enormous blower dryer. What a wonderful man who invented that little gadget!

"Hi, Harry!"

Noel smiled to the greeter. He was her favorite. They all knew her, though—the lonely, crazy girl from the Lower 48 who was always dashing into the store for just a couple of items. Why couldn't she shop all at one time like a normal person? She hadn't figured out what kind of disorder it was, but since her mother and sister did the same, it must be incurable.

Harry smiled back. "Hi, Miss Noel. Did you forget something?" He winked.

"Batteries. And I need some orange juice."

"I heard that. You better keep up on your vitamin C. My wife says it will keep you from catching cold."

"Absolutely! I'm going to do that." Noel waved and turned toward the chilled foods. *Pick up the juice and then grab a pack of batteries close to the checkout counters.*

While she walked, she pondered the plot of her story. There had to be a perfect ending. How could she surprise the reader?

Stopping in front of the juice compartment, she noticed how many of the cartons proudly proclaimed "Florida Orange Juice." It was like a seal of excellence. Okay, she had to work orange juice into the story line. Maybe Richie could buy a grove of oranges or Ellen could be drinking orange juice in the nursing home as she remembered.

Good grief, this is getting bad. Maybe she'd better just trash the whole story.

"Excuse me, do you know if this brand is any good?"

Noel looked up and then looked farther up. The guy was tall and was holding out a carton of orange juice, a question in his eye. But it wasn't the juice that made her stammer. It was what was under his arm. A long-legged, blushing pink, metal flamingo.

She almost giggled.

"Pardon?"

"I know this sounds crazy, but I can't remember which kind of orange juice my mom buys. Do you know what's good?"

"Not crazy. I love good orange juice." Noel held out the carton in her own hand. "This is what I always get, and it's pretty decent. Not quite like fresh-squeezed, but a fair imitation."

"Great." The guy picked up an identical carton.

"I really appreciate this. I'm fixing breakfast in the morning." He grimaced.

Noel knew it was bad manners but said it anyway. "Your wife must really appreciate that."

He met her gaze. "Not my wife, my colleagues. We're from Florida, here on a fishing expedition and taking turns with the meals."

Noel felt foolish. Justifiably so. "Oh." That was that.

She took a step away. "Well, I hope your breakfast turns out well." She was dying to know about the flamingo, but there was no way she was going to stick her neck out twice. The first chop hadn't felt that good.

"Thanks." He turned also. "Hey, wait a minute. There's something else."

Noel swung around.

"I need an honest opinion. Do you like flamingoes?"

No way. A complete stranger asking about. . . flamingoes? "Well, they've never been my favorite bird, but. . ." Noel searched for a way to get out of this tactfully. *Okay, you're a writer; words are your thing. Think!*

He smiled. "Perfect. You said exactly the right thing."

"I did?"

He stuck out his hand. "I'm Richie."

She was going to faint in the juice aisle. "Richie? Are you sure?"

Now he stared at her. "Yeah, last time I checked, it was my name." He grinned. "Is that unusual?"

Just tell him the truth, stupid as it sounds. "You're not going to believe this, but. . ."

He was looking at her with clear blue eyes. Yeah, they were nice. Too bad. She was going to destroy the whole thing right here.

"You see, I'm a writer. And right now, tonight in fact, I'm working on a story called 'The Sign of the Pink Flamingo,' and one of the character's names is Richie and they live in Florida and he goes fishing. So, when I saw that flamingo and heard your name, well that's why I. . ."

He laughed. Really laughed. It was deep and nice. And she laughed with him. What else can you do when you meet a good-looking man in the orange juice section who has a pink flamingo under his arm and smiles when you really botch an introduction?

He shifted the juice in his hand and smiled. "I'm really flattered. And I hope it's a bestselling story."

"Me, too. It probably won't be, though, unless I can think of a decent ending. That's why I'm here. . .to think."

"You think in Walmart?" It was gentle humor.

Noel looked at the ground. "Yeah, a little weird, but lots of times, it works."

"Hey, whatever works, I say. Look. . .I've got a confession. I don't really need orange juice."

"Huh?" Gifted writer that she was, Noel couldn't make the connection.

"I am cooking breakfast in the morning, but none of us drinks orange juice. It was the only thing I could come up with to meet you."

"I don't understand." But Noel's heart was starting

to do the staccato thing.

"I saw you walk in and overheard what you said to the greeter about orange juice. Figured it was as good a place as any to meet you."

"You wanted to meet me?"

"Very much. I've got another confession to make. I've been stalking you."

"What?"

He raised his hand in defense. "I mean, I noticed you in the church I visited last Sunday and well, I'd love to get better acquainted. How about a cup of coffee and a talk?"

Now the heartbeat was definitely intensified, and her face felt warm to boot. But for all that internal action, Noel's tongue was helpless. What does one say at a time like this? What would one of her characters say?

It just popped out. "Richie, do you like road trips?"

He looked puzzled.

"How about slim ankles and steaks with special marinade?"

"I'm not sure I follow the line of thought, but it sounds great to me."

It was her turn to grin. "Yeah, I think Ellen would approve."

"Excuse me?"

"I'll tell you later. And I would love to have coffee. But first, I have to pick up some batteries before I check out."

He pointed into his cart. "I already got 'em. Thought it would save time."

Noel felt a certain kinship to Ellen. Some things must go with the name. He did seem like a Richie.

"Thanks. I guess we can go straight to the checkout then."

"I'm on the way." He stopped suddenly. "Hey, you still haven't told me your name."

"It's Noel. I'm surprised you didn't know it," she teased.

He grinned. "Tried to find out, but couldn't." He stopped in front of the checkout line. "So, shall we go across the street for some coffee now?"

"I'd love to. But first, I have to know, why are you buying a flamingo?"

He stopped the cart and looked at her. "Funny you should ask. Blame that on my grandmother. She said it was important that the right girl for me be honest, and she was crazy about flamingoes—said they were an unknown symbol of undying love. I guess I knew if you would be honest about not liking flamingoes. . . well, let's just say it was my moment of truth. And you know, this pink bird is kind of growing on me. . ."

Noel just smiled. She knew just how she was going to end that story. Tonight, after she enjoyed a cup of coffee with this fascinating man who just might be the one to take road trips to the grandkids with her someday, she'd finish the manuscript and send it off.

"Richie?"

"Yes?"

"Have you ever eaten Jell-O cake?"

"Give, and it will be given to you. They will

pour into your lap a good measure—

pressed down, shaken together, and running over.

For by your standard of measure it will

be measured to you in return."

Luke 6:38 NASB

Used Wisely
David McLaughlan

The theater crowd had just spilled out onto the street. For the past two hours, we had been sitting in plush seats, being wonderfully entertained. Now the still, evening air was full of chatter about the show and what an amazing time everyone had just had. Julie and I were in the middle of it, going with the flow, heading toward the station and the train home.

Then she nudged me and pointed to the edge of the wide sidewalk.

At first I thought he was staff from one of the nearby bars or restaurants putting trash in the Dumpster. He had long, curly, dark hair with flecks of gray through it. Gold-rimmed spectacles rested on his nose. He reminded me of nothing more than the stereotype of a Hebrew scholar. But he wasn't putting stuff in the Dumpster. He was obviously in search of something.

Julie edged me closer.

"Hey," I said as casually as I could. "How you doing there?"

"Just doin' what I need to do to get by," he muttered. He pulled out a french loaf, stuck it in a carrier bag, and went looking for more.

I stood there for a moment, at a loss for what to say next. He steadfastly ignored me and carried on searching. Being watched by me was probably one of the lesser indignities this guy had suffered recently.

"Must be tough," I suggested a little lamely.

I had already spent more than I should have on this lovely night out with my wife. We were only there because the theater was doing a buy-one-get-one-free deal. By most standards I was broke—but then, I wasn't getting my food from a Dumpster.

I had a twenty-pound note in my pocket, about thirty American dollars. I didn't have anything else, so if I was going to help it was that or nothing. My wife, bless her, had already known what I would do when she steered me that way. She also knew we didn't have money to give away, but she wasn't concerned. She's been walking the walk of faith awhile longer than me.

He looked at me for a moment to see if I was serious. "Yeah," he eventually conceded. "Yeah, it is."

"Maybe I can help you a little with that," I said. I held the folded note tucked into my palm as if I was about to shake his hand rather than give him a handout. He knew what I was doing but didn't respond straightaway.

"Are you sure?" he asked.

Strangely, I was sure.

He took the money. Then he looked squarely at me. He didn't say thank you. Instead he said, "I'll use it wisely."

I knew what he was telling me. He was reassuring me he wouldn't blow it on drink or drugs. It's probably the main reason a lot of people don't give money to street beggars, the thought that it might be poured down their necks or injected into their veins. This guy hadn't been begging.

I guessed that someone who *would* spend it on drink or drugs might still say the same thing. But. . .

A while before that I'd been in a similar position.

No, not searching in a Dumpster or living on the streets. I'd been sitting at home on my nice comfy couch, web-surfing with the laptop on my knee. Then a message arrived that put a completely different complexion on my morning.

A friend I've known for some time, someone I know to have a kind heart, told me about a foreign student at her college. This girl had been removed from an abusive family situation by the police and was now in a "safe house." So she was in a strange country, hiding from relatives who beat her, unable to give out her address to any potential friends, and trying to get an education on top of all that.

This girl, perhaps wisely, kept to herself. My friend wanted to help but didn't know how. She assured my friend she was eating but, in stark contrast to that claim, she was getting visibly thinner by the day.

Not having much money herself, my friend had taken to practically forcing sandwiches on this reluctant, but still grateful, girl.

It was none of my business, really. It was hundreds of miles away. Surely the college had contingency funds to help out with situations like that. Oh, I had every excuse in the world not to get involved. But if it had been one of my daughters, would I want other people to hide behind excuses—or help? Besides, this had been put in my way now. Was I going to take up the challenge, or was I going to walk on by?

I checked my meager bank account and withdrew 20 percent of all the money I had. I put it in a pretty card, wrote "A gift of love from God" on the inside, and sealed it. I put that in a bigger envelope with my friend's address on the outside. Then I e-mailed her to warn her what was coming. I asked her to pass it on without giving any clue as to where it had come from.

The mailbox is about a three-minute walk from my house. By the time I had posted the card and walked back, the postman had delivered an envelope to my home. In it was a check I didn't remember being owed—for the same amount I had just sent away!

It's nice to think of such things as divine providence, but in reality I didn't want to be taking money from some earthly organization under false pretences. My reputation and any future business I might do with those people could have been at stake.

I phoned the company that sent it. I was sure they didn't owe me any money. They insisted they did. They couldn't provide any details, but they were certain the payment was mine. So who was I to argue?

My card was still sitting in the postbox. The student who'd been having such a difficult time was still a day or two away from receiving her gift of love. Even so, I had already been thanked! If I had been there as a fly on the wall to see her open that envelope, I couldn't have been more pleased. I'd done a good thing in God's name and been rewarded.

Or had I? Coincidences happen. This could have simply been an amazing example of one. Well, it would have been—if that was the only time anything like that had happened.

A few months later, and I was poor again. (Can you spot a running theme here?) The bills were getting seriously scary. Lack of money was literally keeping me awake at night. Then a big check arrived for some work I had actually done. Great! I started thinking about which bills to pay first.

Say Thank You.

It was just a little voice. I ignored it and turned back to the practicalities. I don't like paying bills usually, but getting these taken care of was going to be a real weight off my mind. But that little voice wouldn't go away. It wasn't loud; it just wasn't going to be ignored.

Say, Thank You, eh?

I remember reading a quote by the monk Meister Eckhart, who said, "If the only prayer you ever pray is, 'Thank You,' it will be enough." Since then, appreciation had been a big part of my prayers.

So I fired up the laptop and electronically zapped some money to a couple of ladies I know who work with orphans and abandoned children in Romania.

This organization, run by a young Californian woman named Sarah and a young German lady named Steffi, does superb work in a hospital in Brasov and out among the Roma (gypsy) communities that live on the fringes of Romanian society.

My daughter had volunteered with them for six months a few years previously. She'd been hugely impressed by the work they did, and I'd kept in touch ever since then. They are in constant need of diaper money, food money, building money, and so on.

Sarah had recently posted a picture on Facebook of a house they built for a Roma family of seven. The walls were rough planks of wood. It was one room with a sloping roof. It stood on four rocks to keep it from soaking up the damp. It was about ten-foot by ten-foot. In the winter it would all but be buried by the Romanian snow. But the family was delighted to have it. It was a big step up from where they had been living before.

I knew they were all volunteers, and I didn't hesitate to help when I could. If I was looking for a way to express my gratitude with a little money, I couldn't think of any better place to send it—or people more desperately in need of it.

The next morning I got an e-mail from Sarah. She explained she'd been in a meeting about a poor Roma family that needed sponsorship. The woman had been abandoned by her husband. She had eight children and no one to help feed them. Romania isn't big on social security for gypsies. Her extended family already existed below the poverty line. There was no one else to help her.

Sarah was pretty sure she could find them a sponsor, but it might take two months to set up. They needed money to tide this family over until the sponsorship kicked in, and their resources were already stretched.

They simply wouldn't turn the woman and her children away, so they did what they do time and again. Everyone at the meeting offered up a prayer.

How much money did they need to feed a family of nine for two months in Romania? Exactly the amount I had sent. When had this meeting taken place and that prayer been sent up? At the same time as I'd been getting urged to say *thank You*.

How does that happen? Well, as Sarah said, "God knows what He's doing."

And He's not stingy about it, either. The next morning another check arrived in the mailbox. Once again it came from a source I didn't think owed me any money. How much? Three times my thank-you!

Back at the Dumpster I thought of all the ways this guy might use the cash I'd just given him. Drink and drugs were the obvious options, but he didn't look the type. He was relatively clean and still had some self-respect about him. Maybe it would get him a bed for the night or food he didn't have to mine from a trash pile. Perhaps he had other plans. Maybe he *would* use it wisely.

In the end it didn't matter. I wasn't called to decide how he spent my gift. I was only called to give. After all, I'd had no control over that banknote before it came to be in my pocket. Why would I think I could control it after it left my possession? What this fellow did with it next was between him and God.

I'd be broke for a while, but I was well used to that. I still got by. I still ate. I had already experienced God's providence in similar times, and I already knew that if you give, you *shall* receive.

He'd told me he would use it wisely. I patted him on the shoulder. "Use it how you like, mate," I said. Then Julie and I went on our way.

The one thing I knew for sure about that twenty-pound note was that in giving it away when I needed it, *I* was the one using it wisely!

For he says, "In the time of my favor I heard you, and in the day of salvation I helped you." I tell you, now is the time of God's favor, now is the day of salvation.

2 Corinthians 6:2 niv

Boiled Peanuts at Midnight

Valorie Quesenberry

It had seemed like such a good idea back home in
Sumner. An offer to spend the year in London, doing
research for the Georgia Historical Society—all expenses
paid with some sightseeing thrown in for good measure.
Jaelynn could still hear Aunt Adele gushing.

"My word, child, what an opportuni–ta! I know
your Mama and Daddy are so proud!" They had been
sitting on the front porch drinking glasses of sweet tea
on a hazy afternoon. The heat was smothering, but the
high ceiling helped and the vintage wicker fans were
keeping the air stirring.

The cicadas buzzed a homey serenade in the dusk
as Jaelynn detailed the offer to her family, bursting
with excitement over her unexpected blessing.
Following her graduate studies at Georgia State, she
had been hired by the Georgia Historical Society,
which was now giving her this once-in-a-lifetime
chance to travel and work. . .on their tab. Her family,
passionate about history in general and family heritage
in particular, was excited with her. Of course she
should go. After all, it was only for a year, and think
what she could see and do and learn along the way.
Wouldn't Gramps and Granny Windsor have been
proud? After all, they were descended from English

aristocracy who had taken their place in the society of plantation owners when America was only an infant country.

While the moon rose on their sleepy Southern town, Jaelynn and her family talked and laughed and dreamed about what the next year would hold for her.

But now as she sat in a cubbyhole in front of a computer with rain pouring outside, she was having a hard time dredging up that same excitement. She loved the work; following trails of historical facts, discovering ties between the known and the unknown—she could immerse herself for hours. But, when the workday ended and it was time to return to her small flat on a London side street, she missed her Georgia roots desperately.

"Nasty day, what?"

Jaelynn looked up to meet the merry eyes of a coworker. Malcolm Pipstreet was classically British. He had sandy hair, a regal nose, a neatly trimmed mustache, and a dapper attitude. He didn't look a bit of his fifty-five years. He claimed a Yorkshire terrier and a parakeet as house companions. And contrary to the long-standing joke about the English, he possessed a ready wit and could have her smiling in seconds.

"You said it. At home, we would call this a gully washer."

Malcolm leaned his elbows on the divider of her cubby. "I say, that's a delightful way to put it. Rather a bit more colorful than simply a rainstorm. Dreadful weather, all the same."

"But I thought Londoners were used to rain?"

"Rain, yes, my dear. But not this tempest brewing outside." He gestured to the window where lightning jagged the sky. "I think I shall spend the evening by the fire with the poet for company."

She grinned. "Shelley or Keats?"

"Possibly Shakespeare. Good for the mind; none of this frothy fiction." He tapped his pencil on the novel lying on her desk and walked off.

In spite of her melancholy, Jaelynn smiled. She so enjoyed their friendly banter.

She clicked the mouse to open the next file on the menu. It was a particularly interesting topic— "Letters to England from the South during the War of Northern Aggression." Jaelynn could see Southern fingerprints all over this file; only folks from Dixie used that title for the Civil War.

She grabbed her coffee mug and sat back to read.

February 1865

Dearest Corlene,

I take my pen in hand to inform you of my health and recent activities. I suppose you hear news of the war there in Berkshire, but I wonder if they truly report the dreadful facts as they are. . . .

Oh, Corlene, I cannot find the words to describe to you the absolute destruction left in

[General Sherman's] wake! Many estates of our friends and neighbors are lying in ruin, their stately pillars crumbling and scorched by fire. The fields are barren as if a swarm of locusts had descended in rage upon them. The towns are pitiful and little children are starving and their mothers have descended so low as to butcher anything that moves upon the ground to keep them alive until their fathers return in glory. . . .

Yet, we fare far better than many. We have tried to be as generous as we can, but if the masses know of our remaining food, we should be swarmed with the hungry, and I fear then for the lives of any.

I hear that the soldiers have taken to eating peanuts in great quantity. With the fields burned, food for our brave men is scarce. In peanuts, they have found a ready source for their appetite. They have even taken to eating the goobers boiled over a fire with a bit of salted meat thrown in for flavor.

Naturally, I thought of you and our cooking experiments as girls. We still have a goodly portion of peanuts here at Heatherton, so I had Jolie boil some up with a bit of our salt. I must tell you, Corlene, that I was quite dubious of the taste, as privation could cause soldiers to prevaricate about the goodness of their diet. To my surprise, I found that I quite liked them. The shell becomes soft so they can be opened easily. Their taste reminds me of the pinto beans we often have with cornpone. And the salt gives the whole experience a pleasurable dimension. I wonder if my John is now eating them, too. The other day I heard our soldiers referred to as "goober grabbers." May God have pity on them; they are such brave men.

I have enclosed a small package of our dry Georgia peanuts with this letter, Corlene. Though you are in the land of abundance with our Aunt Josephine and have ample nutrition, I wanted to send you a gift to remind you of your great Southern heritage. You may boil them in some brine and try this new dish that has become a staple here at home. I await your opinion with anticipation.

Write when you can. The winter days are long, though spring approaches soon. We hope to quickly see an end to this conflict and a return to the former days of peace and prosperity.

May God keep you, dearest sister.
Lovingly, Emma

Jaelynn's coffee had grown cold, but she took a reflexive taste anyway. The letter was amazing—such insight into the Civil War era as well as being particularly pleasing to her with Georgia being her home state.

She grabbed a pencil and legal pad to jot down initial thoughts for later research. She felt a sense of kinship with these sisters, one so far from home and in England, no less.

The time on her desk clock read five minutes until closing. She put her notebook into a drawer, arranged the items on her desk, and powered down her work computer. In the morning, she would do an advanced search of the files to find any other letters from Emma Heatherton Cooper.

On the way home, Jaelynn stopped at a marvelous little shop for fish and chips (such an odd name for french fries). She found a table in the corner and listened to the voices around her as she ate. She had discovered that no matter which side of the ocean one was on, people and relationships and families were basically the same. The cultures were different, but under the skin, everyone had needs and fears, joys and triumphs. It reminded her of the last sermon she had heard Pastor Tredell preach before she left home. One particular part was imprinted in her memory.

"This world belongs to our God, every inch. The people in it are His creation and no matter where we are, we are within view of His loving eye and hand of mercy. He is everywhere."

She was sure he spoke the truth.

Jaelynn left the shop and headed for the tube station. Riding on London's subway system was so intriguing for a history buff. It was in these underground caverns that Londoners hid while Nazi bombers ravaged their city. She thought of it every time she stepped into a train for her commute.

Her flat was on Wellington Drive, a typical British street. In the foyer of the weathered stone building, there was a tall brass container for umbrellas, that ubiquitous accessory of every good Londoner. She placed her own flowered one in it. There was a code among the residents—a person's umbrella was sacred property; it was never stolen.

Jaelynn started toward the lift entrance (it even sounded normal now to use that word for the elevator). Passing the row of mailboxes, she noticed a package in her mail space. She pulled it out, surprised at its weight. The return address was Atlanta, Georgia, United States. All the way to the second floor, she tried to guess its contents.

Inside her flat, Jaelynn kicked off her shoes, sank into a chintz armchair, and opened the package. A letter fell out. It was from her sister, Jocelyn.

Dear Jae,

I imagine you're tired after a day's work of research. Knowing you, you're probably putting in extra hours most days. I'm so happy that you are doing what you love, but I miss you terribly. Weekends at home in Sumner just aren't the same without you. Aunt Adele says that when you left the "light went right out of Dixie." I guess

I'd have to agree.

I won't go on very long since I can write longer letters by e-mail than longhand. (Wouldn't Miss Prentiss from Sumner High have a fit about my cursive?) But I wanted to send you a taste of home and had to put a note in with it. I've figured up the travel time and think you should be getting this by Thursday. I hope it's not too heavy to carry to your room. The canned ones aren't nearly as good as the fresh ones from Hill's Farm Stand, but they'll have to do. I know how much you love them.

I'll be having some myself for the next few nights, probably around at 8:00 when I'm done with the evening routine here at the library. If you want to join me, we'll call this a long-distance sisterly snack, okay?

Much love always,
Jocie

P.S. At home last weekend, I found something you should research. Mama gave me a packet of letters to an Emma Heatherton Cooper, an ancestor of ours. It seems she had a sister in England, too, at one point. Thought you might run across something about her. Let me know.

Jaelynn pulled back the packaging to reveal ten cans of boiled peanuts. It must have cost Jocelyn a fortune to send something so heavy.

She held one up to her cheek. "Thanks, sis. What a perfect gift."

The time difference between London and Georgia meant that 8 p.m. in Atlanta would be 12 a.m. here. Who cared? That would give her time to do some further research on her laptop about Emma Heatherton Cooper. Just wait until she told Jocelyn about that coincidence. In fact, it wouldn't surprise her at all to discover that Emma and Corlene had also shared a long-distance sisterly snack like she and Jocelyn. And Jaelynn was sure that nothing would taste any better to two sisters than boiled peanuts at midnight.

"For nothing will be
impossible with God."

LUKE 1:37 NASB

Coincidence

Paul Muckley

Do you believe in coincidence?

Before you answer, consider this story of a new family and a used van. The story is 100 percent true— only the names have been changed, as they say, to protect the innocent.

Self-assessment would have plopped Lynne and me squarely into the "young couple" category. But we weren't really *that* young—she was thirty-two, I was thirty-three. Married for nine years, we only heard the pitter-patter of little feet at home when our two cats were on the prowl.

Of course, we wanted kids. But the doctor could never pinpoint why they didn't come. Officially, we were experiencing an "unexplained infertility."

The good news was that it wasn't my fault, nor was it Lynne's. But that little pat on the back didn't put a baby in the nursery. Fertility treatments followed, though only for a few frustrating and expensive months. Adoption, always a hazy possibility, soon sharpened into our preferred option.

Lynne and I are both white, but when we learned that the agency we'd chosen wanted prospective parents for its "transracial" program, we quickly signed on for any biracial baby that might come along. And, relatively quickly, one did. We learned about Hialeah a little more than a week before she was due.

Our "nine-day pregnancy" flew by, a week and two days of mad scrambling to prepare a nursery and buy baby clothes, diapers, bottles, medicines—you name it. For a while, we felt like we were single-handedly pushing the national economy in a nifty new stroller.

And then came the phone call—our baby had been born!

Most nights are far too short. This one felt like a year. But the morning finally arrived, and we were soon making a ninety-minute drive to the hospital to meet our birth mom, Kelsey. Hialeah was resting in the neonatal intensive care unit while doctors observed a breathing problem. If all went well with Kelsey, we'd get to see the baby later that day.

Things went very well. Kelsey was a quiet, serious young woman in her early twenties, and we felt a quick connection with her. Her upbringing had been far less than ideal, but she was trying to make something of her life by enrolling in classes at a nearby community college. Kelsey was hoping, someday, to be a professional chef.

She already had a three-year-old daughter, Aria, and knew it would be very difficult to handle a second baby on her own. As with every good mom, Kelsey wanted a better opportunity for Hialeah, and—

excruciating as the decision was for her—knew she had to place the baby up for adoption.

Our visit lasted more than two hours. We talked about where we'd all come from and where we hoped to go in life. We discussed our parenting philosophies and our plans for our families. We soon felt like old friends.

And then Kelsey made the announcement that would literally change our lives: she wanted *us* to parent Hialeah.

So it was finally time to meet this kid.

Kelsey, Lynne, and I walked together to the NICU. It was a serious place, with some gravely ill babies fighting for their health—and in some cases, their lives—amid brightly colored decorations put up by the nursing staff. Though Hialeah had problems, they weren't considered life threatening.

A nurse pointed us to Hialeah's area. There, partially hidden by breathing tubes, monitor wires, and the plastic cover of her sterile bassinet, lay the most beautiful baby we'd ever seen. Her cocoa skin and shock of shiny, dark hair literally took my breath away—a quick gasp, followed by the conscious decision to breathe again. And that was before I'd even caught my first glimpse of her stunning brown eyes.

Call it a cliché, but there was magic in the air. And there was magic in our first touch, even if that came through a rubber glove attached to the bassinet cover.

Hialeah's heartbeat and breathing were racing, as we could clearly see on the monitor over her bed. But they each calmed dramatically when I laid my hand on her little body.

Hialeah spent a week in that hospital, and so did Lynne. The medical staff allowed Lynne to stay in a small dorm-like room that had once housed nursing students, so she could both learn the care of a newborn and help out with the same.

My employer, a book publisher, gave me freedom to come and go as needed that week, so I generally worked until early afternoon then drove an hour and a half to visit "my girls." Lynne was holding, feeding, and changing Hialeah each day, and as the week went on, I did, too. And I found that diapers weren't quite as frightening as I'd earlier thought.

Hialeah grew stronger and stronger, slowly but surely shedding the various wires and tubes she'd been sporting. I was most pleased when the nurses finally removed an intravenous line stuck directly into our daughter's forehead.

When the doctor announced that we could take Hialeah home the next day, it struck me that we still needed a baby seat for the car. That was easily enough remedied at the big-box baby store on the way home, which happened to be holding a baby-seat safety check that day. You can bet those checkers heard the whole story of our little girl!

I returned to the hospital the next morning, on a very chilly late September day. We thanked the nurses and said good-bye. We thanked Kelsey—though that seemed pitifully inadequate for the gift she'd given us—and said good-bye. And we carried Hialeah in her brand-new punkin seat to our little blue Chevy Cavalier, legally waiting in the "patient pick-up" lane.

If you're familiar with vehicle makes, you'll recognize the Cavalier as a "compact car." That means it's small. And our two-door model posed a few challenges to situating a baby carrier in the cramped backseat.

We worked with that for a while, but it didn't take long for all the head-bumpings and back-wrenchings to get us thinking about a more family-friendly vehicle. Now what says "family" more than a minivan? We started visiting used car lots in search of a vehicle upgrade.

Before long, a green Dodge Caravan caught Lynne's eye. It *was* pretty sharp—with paint stripes and body skirting that made it much sportier than most of its minivan cousins. It was definitely used, with eighty-some thousand miles under its frame. But the price was right, and we knew we could grow into the vehicle. Hialeah was never intended to be an only child.

Financing came through the Bank of Mom—Lynne's mom, who withdrew some cash out of a retirement account. Our plan was to pay her back as quickly as possible, starting with whatever we received in a royalty check, due in about five months.

I've mentioned my job with a book publisher. As an editor, I would generally pass judgment on other people's writing—as proposals that arrive through the mail or as manuscripts that I've contracted and received from authors. But a couple of years earlier, I'd jumped the fence and obtained a contract for a book of my own. Not the great American novel, but a book of Bible trivia. Though we never expected that book to make us rich, Lynne and I did plan to put the income it generated toward building our family. And stepping up from a tiny car to a van was one part of that plan.

My book was relatively small and inexpensive, the royalty rate modest. Averaged over all the various sales channels, each copy sold would yield roughly a dime.

But God was good and the book was popular. In its first year, more than two hundred thousand copies sold, and the resulting royalty—a little over twenty thousand dollars—covered the costs of Hialeah's adoption. Believe me, we were thankful. In the early years of our marriage, finding several thousand dollars for an adoption would have been more than daunting—it would have been nearly impossible.

But those days were behind us now. We'd brought Hialeah into our home, finalized the adoption in court at the six-month mark, and thrilled to every tiny thing she learned and did. If you have kids, you know what I mean—all those things that every baby on earth learns and does, but that seem utterly miraculous when they happen to yours.

Since she was able to stay home with Hialeah, Lynne saw almost everything first—the first time the baby rolled over, the first time she sat by herself, the first time she ate solid food. But I like to claim Hialeah's first real smile.

Maybe she appreciated me as the family's provider. I kept on editing books, critiquing others' writing while casting an occasional eye over the sales of my own. That Bible trivia kept selling, and those dimes kept adding up. Not long after Hialeah's first professional portrait at five months, my annual book accounting would come due.

Generally, the skill sets of editors and accountants don't overlap very much, and that was certainly true in my case. I had only a very rough idea of what payment to expect, and hoped—without any real evidence— that it would be large enough to pay off our entire van loan at once.

Royalty reports carry all kinds of information— like the number of copies sold, to which markets, at what discounts, before how many returns come back to the publisher's warehouse. But my guess is that ninety-nine out of every one hundred writers look immediately to a single section of the printout—the one that reads "Total earnings this period." I know that's where I always went first.

Would it be enough to retire the loan?

Let's see. . .

$10,644.04.

Hey, cool. . .it is enough!

But, wait a minute. . .

Why does that number seem so familiar?

Ten thousand, six hundred forty-four.

I know I've seen that number somewhere before.

Hmmm. . .

No way. . .

Could it be?

Downstairs to the old metal filing cabinet, and pull out the top drawer—the one that screeches horribly ever since the little plastic rollers fell off. Thumb though the folders and grab the one labeled "Automotive."

Inside, there's a bill of sale for our green Dodge Caravan. Sale price, tax, title, and all other expenses total—you guessed it—$10,644.00.

Coincidence?

Not in our minds. We prefer to think of that as a God-thing.

Now, some people might quibble over the additional four cents on the royalty check. If it's really a God-thing, why wouldn't those figures be exact to the penny?

But we chose not to worry over that.

The spare change went into Hialeah's college savings account.

Above all, love each other deeply, because love covers over a multitude of sins.

1 PETER 4:8 NIV

The Tree

Shelley R. Lee

Sitting on the porch steps under a pastel summer sunset, I noticed how big one of the trees had gotten.

It took me back to that spring that we had planted it. One of my best friends was going to plant that tree in her yard. How I got it is part of this story.

The first time I met her was at her wedding on a date with my would-be husband, Dave, her husband's cousin. I had never seen such pure and simple beauty, in a person or a ceremony. And if that wasn't captivating enough, they rode off in a horse and buggy on that beautiful day.

She was magnetic and genuine. I soon looked forward to in-law gatherings because I would get to see Kim. With each family gathering, we became better friends. By the time Dave and I were married and had baby Trevor, in Michigan, Dave had gotten a teaching job back home in Ohio where Kim and Gary lived.

I dreaded the move initially. It meant leaving some very good Christian friends who were instrumental in my renewed faith in God. I was in a spiritually good place in Michigan. I was just sure there would be no Christians in Ohio! Of course the big U of M–Ohio

State rivalry goes into play here, but that's an entirely different story. I was incredibly sad to leave Michigan. Home.

Then I thought of Kim, and there was excitement in my heart. Of course the rest is history as they say. And here is where the history is recorded. Kim and Gary were such a blessing to us. I didn't know where to begin with the process of finding a place to live. Kim spearheaded the project. She gathered the local classifieds—the Internet was not even heard of yet— and highlighted several possibilities that might fit. Then the five of us headed out, apartment hunting together. What seemed scary to me at the outset became joyful. She had a way of doing that.

She found us an apartment in the small town of McComb a few miles from their farm, where we would live for the next few years.

Kim grew the most beautiful plants and flowers that this novice gardener had ever seen. "Would you like to take home some peonies?" she would ask me every spring. But the question was really more a formality, being that she was already preparing a moist paper towel in a plastic bag for the freshly cut flowers. They were the biggest, most lush flowers I had seen in my life. I felt like a queen taking them home with me.

As I was loading up kids and flowers to head home from her house one day, I was struck by the rich, colorful flowers along the sidewalk. "What are those called?" I asked.

"Moss roses," she said with such satisfaction.

One afternoon Kim invited me over to watch *Somewhere in Time*, a Christopher Reeve movie. In the enchanting film, a photo of his future love interest (played by Jane Seymour), attracts him beyond reason. We learn later that as the photo was taken she was looking lovingly at him. (This occurred in the past but at a later date. . .there was a bit of time travel involved. You must watch the movie!) It was a fabulous afternoon! We ate delicious frozen pizza bread in her kitchen with a view of her magnolia tree in magnificent full bloom.

One spring Kim and Gary planted hundreds of pine trees to use as Christmas trees in the future. A whole field of trees, and they watered them all. But the tree in my front yard still wasn't planted yet.

Kim also introduced me to *Anne of Green Gables*. So fitting, because she and I were kindred spirits like the girls in the movie. In those years of young womanhood, we encouraged each other in the struggles of making marriage work and raising children well. We grew in our faith, sharpening each other along the way. But I'm jumping ahead in the story.

I can't forget the early years, when I had the only child. We frequently went over on weekends to their peaceful farm and enjoyed bonfires with little Trevor and her beloved bassett hound, Calliope.

One day we went shopping and between stops sat in the parking lot for a long time while she poured out her heart about concern for not being able to get pregnant. By this time I was pregnant with our second child. But Kim was gracious and full of faith; she was willing to accept whatever God gave her.

By late summer that year, we had Hannah and she rejoiced with us. Then grieved with us when she and Gary were the first loved ones to arrive after we found our infant daughter dead one fall morning from SIDS. Kim supported me in great ways that difficult season.

A nurse, she always loved her work. So when she got pregnant she wondered how she would do balancing work and motherhood. But soon after having Josh she said, "I never knew just how much I would love being a mother." She held him with sweet affection, looking straight into his eyes. That year we each had little boys, six months apart.

Less than a couple of years later we each had another boy within months of each other—I had Westley, she had Matthew.

Sometime that following year we were sitting on my porch swing at our little house in Cygnet, Ohio, holding children and watching the older ones play. Kim asked me if I were to have another daughter, if I would not use the name Megan. She wanted a Megan, she told me excitedly.

Sometime in the next year I had my fourth son, Dexter, and she had Megan.

We were done having children, and we each needed bigger homes for them. Within a year of one another we each built homes twenty minutes from one another, in different school districts. Theirs, in a big, beautiful wooded lot; ours next to a river and little wooded gully. We helped one another a lot, as we had for many home improvement projects over the years. Dave and Gary did a lot of roofing together. One day Kim and I sat on scaffolding, just the two of us, siding the north side of my house all afternoon. We talked the entire time and got a lot of work done.

But that tree still wasn't planted in my front yard.

After all the hard work we had done, we enjoyed time visiting at one another's homes and letting the kids play while we visited in the moments we had. Kim observed one day, sitting in my floral dining room, how very different our styles were. She was very country; I leaned toward Victorian. She commented on how fun it was that we were different in that way, but enjoyed the beauty of one another's homes very much.

I enjoyed hosting ladies' tea parties in those days, Victorian style, and Kim and her mother, Shirley, attended one of them together on a summer day. I had asked one or two of the husbands to be "butlers" for us, and we all got dressed up. It was such great fun! I was going around getting pictures of everyone. Kim stood in my kitchen, and her eyes lit up as she looked at me as I took the photo. It ended up being the best photo I had seen of her. It was a nice memento of that enjoyable time with good friends.

The flowers were beautifully in bloom, but that tree still wasn't in the ground.

The following spring Kim and Gary and the kids came over, and she made Flubber for all the kids. She had the recipe (that could also be found on what was called the *Internet*?). The kids loved it and laughed so hard at the funny oozing substance. It was a really fun night for all of us.

Still no tree. We're getting there. . . .

A few weeks later I came home from work and found a phone message from a family member. "I'm sorry to tell you this way, but Kim has been life-flighted to the hospital. She has an aneurysm." I collapsed onto my counter in shock, crying and gasping, and then called my neighbor to ask if she would drive with me to the hospital. I was in no state to drive.

My neighbor, Sarah, led the way. I was in a daze. I could not have asked where the ICU was without breaking down. When we got up to her room they took me in to see her. I cannot get her intense brown eyes out of my mind. They had immobilized her and given her pain medication. I went right up to her face, and her eyes locked on mine and told me volumes in a single look. She knew me. She had her mind; that was very clear.

I sat with Gary and the family, and the neurological surgeon explained what he would be doing, the risks, and how long recovery might take if things went as planned. We all sat there stunned. *She may never be the same,* I realized.

The next day they took her into surgery, but before she went she asked Gary to videotape her singing "Jesus Loves You" to her children—just in case.

Less than a week later I stood at her graveside on a beautiful grassy hill under a mighty oak tree. Life Flight sent one of their choppers to do a salute during the ceremony. I had never seen a helicopter bow down before. As if I needed something more to weep about. The big church where we came from was packed to standing room only, speaking more volumes about the impact her life had on so many people.

Gary came over with the kids a week or two later. "I have some trees," he said. He and Kim had bought several trees they were going to plant. But now he figured he would share some of them with the people who missed her. He gave us one that looks like a pine but drops its needles in the winter. I obviously never got as good at gardening as Kim was; I don't even know the name of the tree.

Sometime after the tree was planted, Gary called. They were working on her gravestone and wanted a photo of her on it. Her mom, Shirley, loved the photo of Kim that I took at the tea party and asked if I had the negative.

In a dream I had of Kim after she died, she was gardening in summer overalls, warm sand beneath her bare feet, in what seemed like my front yard (or maybe I just wanted to believe it was my front yard, but it was my dream). She wouldn't speak; she merely stood there smiling and motioning excitedly for me to come and help her. There was a lot of gardening to be done. I was so sad to wake up from that dream.

On occasion, when I'm troubled, I drive out to that grassy hill under the mighty oak and I see Kim smiling at me, just like in *Somewhere in Time*. That seems like no coincidence to me. It's a gift.

Everything about her was a gift.

As I sat on the porch steps marveling at the tree, I recalled sitting in that very spot several years ago now, mourning and bewildered at the loss of my dear friend, staring at the newly planted tree.

Today it is growing strong and beautiful, just like her.

Today I take life's gardening more seriously. I think about who needs a little seed of hope, who needs a little more sunshine or water. And maybe someday I will be strong and beautiful, like her. Branching out and growing into the wide open spaces, roots deep in what is true, good, and eternal.

May the God of hope fill you with all joy and peace as you trust in him, so that you may overflow with hope by the power of the Holy Spirit.

ROMANS 15:13 NIV

The Honeymoon's Over, Mostly

Maura Klopfenstein Oprisko

Everything. I could smell everything. I could smell the tomatoes a room away; I could smell the dust on the TV; I could smell. . .whatever our couch smelled like, and I was valiantly fighting the urge to use the bucket by my head.

I knew Will was tired of this, and I was embarrassed, but completely helpless to stop it. Any minute now, he would come home to find this unshowered, emaciated wife just as he left me this morning. He'd give me a kiss on the forehead, ask me how I was feeling, and then go clean up the cutting board covered in dried-up tomato seeds. Tomatoes were all I could eat. Weird, I know. When I went to cut one up an hour ago, I blacked out in the August sunlight that was relentlessly pouring through the kitchen window, and I caught myself on a chair just in time. So, I found refuge once again on the couch, with my head inches away from the air conditioner, while the tomato mess dripped everywhere and began to dry.

And he would miss *SG-1* again tonight. There was no way I could get up from the couch ever again. I was sure of it. And, though I might've sucked up my passionate hatred of all things science fiction for an hour so he could watch his one and only show, he was being careful these days. Or something. I'm not sure what it was exactly. Maybe he felt bad for me in my violent illness and didn't want to make me watch something I hated. Maybe he was watching it in our bedroom, relishing the time away from his lump of a wife. I didn't know. But I was a little nervous that he wasn't pleased with this marriage he'd gotten himself into just two months ago.

This wasn't supposed to happen now. He'd moved from Indiana to Cleveland for me. He wasn't crazy about it here, but when he did it, he knew he was about to propose and had my dire job situation in mind. He wanted me to have a chance at finding work once we got married and I moved in. I'd already spent two years living with my parents, just an hour and a half south of Cleveland, and had worked tirelessly trying to find work, to no avail. He knew, at this point, that my only chance was to be in a bigger city, and it made sense for him to be closer to me during our engagement than the six hours we were used to. So, he picked up all his belongings and set up camp in a city he didn't even like. For me. And then, almost as soon as we came home from our honeymoon and I'd moved in, it was this. It ruined everything.

—

"Where are you going?" he asked, turning around from the kitchen cabinets, his mouth full of peanuts.

I squeezed my eyes shut. "Oh, come on! You couldn't have waited till the second month of marriage to talk with your mouth full?"

"Nope," he said, smiling widely with peanutty teeth and leaning in for a kiss.

I shoved his face away with my hand, laughing. "Gross, weirdo! I'm going to the drugstore," I said. "I'll be back in a minute. I'm just going to the one on North Park."

" 'Kay," he said, turning back around. And I closed the door behind me.

I let my smile drop. I didn't want him to know—mostly because it was stupid, and it would just freak him out. I'd go get the test, take it in secret, then show him the negative result, and we'd both laugh. He would ask me why in the world I thought I was pregnant, to which I'd say I don't know—I felt funny. Probably just paranoid. We couldn't have a baby right now. Now, I always knew that children were a blessing from God. But it was a blessing I'd rather have gone without until I was thirty. I had too many things to do right now to have kids. I had a career to start. I had college loans to pay down. No, you don't understand—I was twenty-four years old and carried $60,000 worth of debt into my marriage. I had all my belongings to unpack still, for crying out loud. Oh, and we lived in an apartment in a college dormitory. You heard me. Will's job was in residence life, so we actually lived in the dorm. Bottom line: the day we got married, when the inevitable jerk or two made comments on how we would surely come home from our honeymoon with a baby on the way (probably because that's how they did it), we had no time for it. It wasn't funny. We'd respond with a curt, "no," and change the subject. We did *not* want kids. Not for years.

I knew twenty minutes from now I'd be completely relieved. I thought about Will giving me grief about it for years to come. Every time I'd complain about an upset tummy or a very pungent smell from now on, he'd tease me that I'm pregnant, and I'd slap his arm. And then, someday, a long time from now, we'd say, "Hey, let's have a baby."

I stood in front of the selection of tests, not even really knowing why I was doing this. I knew I felt "funny," and really tired. I probably just hadn't had enough protein or something this week, and I'd be mad at myself tomorrow for wasting the twelve bucks. *I'm not even that late,* I thought. *And I have cramps already.* I grabbed the one with the most tests in it, forked over everything in my wallet, and stuffed the paper bag in my purse. As I walked away, the cashier called after me, "Hey, good luck!" I smiled at her weakly, thinking that was the perfect thing to say.

But I never had to wait the two minutes. As long as it took me to administer the test and raise it to my eye level was all the time it took for the little plus sign to show up, but I think I just sat there and stared at it forever. I hadn't considered this. *Pregnant. I'm actually pregnant. Not paranoid. Pregnant.* Becoming parents wasn't "someday" anymore. It was inevitable. It was. . . now.

I stepped out of the bathroom. Then, I chickened out and dove back inside. Deep breath. I reemerged. "Honey?" I called.

He was fussing with our broken fan in the living room, but when he heard the tone of my voice and saw which room I was leaving, he froze. He knew. I didn't even have to say anything else.

"You're pregnant," he said quietly. There was no question.

I nodded, grimacing.

He'd taken a seat on the couch. I sank into the cushion next to him and irreverently tossed the positive test on the coffee table. The rest of the night, we went back and forth between crying devastated tears and sitting frozen in stunned silence.

The cramps didn't go away over the next few days—they got worse. So, I took the remaining tests in the box, thinking that perhaps the first one was a fluke. How great would it be if it were just a bad test? That would solve everything. I could get back to unpacking, salvaging our dorm apartment into some semblance of a home. . . . I could get back to my job hunt. But no. Three more tests yielded positive results, and as the hours went by, the pain in my abdomen doubled me over. It was excruciating.

I called Will at work. No answer. I called his cell. Nothing. I called my family doctor two hours away, who told me either to see my OB-GYN or the emergency room immediately. I had no OB-GYN in town yet, so I grabbed a phone book and started with the *As*. Nobody was nice, nobody was taking new patients, and everyone said to get to the emergency room—*yesterday*. I dialed Will again.

"Where. . .in the. . .*world*. . .have you been?" I snapped, when I heard his unsuspecting voice. "I've been trying to reach you. . . ."

"I was in a meeting! What? What's going on?"

"You need to come home and take me to the hospital. I've never had cramps like this; it's like I—"

"I'll be right there."

Click.

After nine hours in the emergency room, several needle pokes, a painful IV, and another positive pregnancy test (no, really?), we were in the ultrasound room, waiting for the technician to tell us whether or not our baby was being miscarried.

We weren't looking at each other. The room was just heavy with silence, and I thought maybe he was mad at me. Maybe he thought this was my fault, maybe I misinterpreted something a doctor said once about fertile weeks, or maybe I forgot to take my temperature once, or. . .I don't know. But I felt desperate. I wanted so much for him to say something. Or even just look at me, give me a reassuring smile.

I tried to distract myself by calling to mind the million times we were asked today whether or not we'd had a difficult time conceiving. Mostly, we'd looked at them like they had rotten meat on their faces. It would probably be funny someday, but in the moment, I just wanted to tell them to go walk down one of their crazy-twisty hallways and get themselves lost.

My reverie came to an abrupt end when a perky, ponytailed nurse bounded into the room. "Hey, guys!" she exclaimed. Her voice was jarring. It kind of reminded me of being a fifth-grade camper and waking to the sound of trumpets.

She flipped on the ultrasound machine, got out the scanner, and ran it over my belly, looking for the baby. And then. . .

"There's the start of your baby!" First Trumpet proclaimed, pointing at a white speck. We stared at the screen, dumbstruck. I felt Will's hand on mine.

She spoke up again. "You're not miscarrying," she said. A bunch of air escaped my lips. Relief? Surprised at myself, I looked up at my husband, and there it was. His smile. I grasped his hand back. Hard.

"But I can tell you what's causing you all that pain," she continued. "You have a cyst. A big one, too.

Wow, I bet that hurts."

"Is that serious?" Will asked.

"No," she said, "and the baby should be fine, too. The cyst will rupture by itself, and don't worry. . .baby won't mind that either. But it'll probably feel like your muscles are tearing when it happens."

"Awesome," I replied, still studying the little white, flickering speck.

She took a few pictures and printed them out. There in my hands was a picture of our baby. Our *baby*. For the first time, it didn't completely freak me out.

I looked at Will. "We're gonna have a baby, hon."

He hadn't stopped looking at me and smiling. "I know," he said simply and kissed me.

—

I thought it was the TV that woke me up, but when I opened my eyes, I saw Will shuffling around in the kitchen. "Honey, I brought you home some penne," he called.

"Thanks," I said. "That sounds good, actually."

He dragged tired feet through the living room and dropped himself onto the couch next to me, a plastic container and fork in hand. "I thought it might," he said. "Tomatoes, marinara. . .you know." He pointed the fork at me, poised to feed me.

"So what are we watching, here?" he asked.

I bit the penne off the fork and turned around to

look at the clock. "Latht week'ph *SG-1* iv on in ten minuteth," I said, turning back toward him, mouth full. His forehead and chin puckered in disgust, so I gave him my biggest marinara smile and flipped to the SyFy channel.

Don't worry about anything;

instead, pray about everything.

Tell God what you need,

and thank him for all he has done.

Philippians 4:6 nli

What a Great Idea!

Kathy Douglas

My husband and I are ideally suited, but not because he's my Ideal Man. Idealism wilts like old lettuce when one marries not the Ideal Man, but an *Idea* Man. This is my story, and I'm not making up a word of it.

Some women claim they married the Right Man. Others moan they married the Wrong Man. Still others admit to having married the Boy Next Door or their High School Sweetheart. Some might boast that they did, in fact, marry the Ideal Man. (Those who make that boast include women who have been married for less than fifty minutes or for more than fifty years.) For those of us who have married Idea Men instead of Ideal Men, one letter does not the only difference make.

My first whispered warning that my Ideal Man was an Idea Man came the third time I saw him extract a large wad of cash from his pocket to pay for our date. My Idea Man's sense of humor was what initially captured my heart—not his money. He won me over making me laugh. To this day my heart wears a smiley face most of the time.

When he pulled out a fistful of bills on that memorable third date, however, I decided, *Bonus! This guy is flush with cash!* Our courtship held promise independent of money, but this unexpected display of wealth got me thinking. *Maybe I can be a stay-at-home wife and mother. Wouldn't that be great?* Not suspecting my own self-delusion, I smiled to myself. *He* is *ideal!*

Cash, I learned as our love and relationship progressed, was how this man paid for almost everything. That's why he had so much on hand. His idea? The smart guy pays as he goes with no middleman to muck things up.

When we began dating over thirty years ago, credit cards were just starting to wheedle their indispensable presence into the American wallet. Internet banking was the stuff of sci-fi enthusiasts. Back then everyone— everyone—myself included, had a checking account. As archaic as that sounds now, that was how most of us paid for utilities, rent, and dates. Not my Idea Man.

Cash or a cashier's check was his modus operandi. He didn't like banks. He didn't trust banks. He still doesn't. His idea, since the time he could spell the word *bank*, is that banks can't be trusted with anyone's money but their own. That should have alerted me that life married to an Idea Man, even if he were my ideal, would be somewhat atypical. My Idea Guy, like all Idea Men, lives in a different reality than the rest of us.

Not only do Idea Men think differently than the rest of us, they do things differently than most of us, too. My Idea Guy did things his way. Call an appliance repairman for a failing refrigerator? Call a plumber for a leaky faucet? Get the name of a good mechanic to tinker with the car? No way!

His idea was to always try his hand at a project first. He tackled problems or projects on his own. I grew more convinced that he was my Ideal Man: thrifty, smart, independent, industrious. I was impressed—and smitten.

When we spoke our vows, I stood assured the gentleman beside me was my Ideal Man. Frankly, I still didn't get it. I was marrying, first and foremost, an Idea Man. Soon my newlywed idealism lay mangled under the advancing parade of my husband's new or better ideas. I began to realize I had snuggled in with an Idea Man for life.

One day my Idea Man announced we should move to the country. Why someone used to the convenience of city living desired relocation to country *inconvenience* mystified our friends. I was somewhat mystified myself, but the Idea Guy assured me this was a great idea.

"Let the naysayers be hanged," he said. "We're moving out!"

Construction of a new home, I soon learned, fans an Idea Man's creative spark into wildfire. In keeping with his idea-ism, my Idea Guy did most of the work. Electrical, plumbing, central vacuuming—what he tackled was as impressive as the finished product. He amazed me along every step of the way—just like he had before we were married. My love and admiration deepened for my mate, this near genius. I allowed myself to relax about his big idea, our move to the country.

We started moving items from our city house to our new country home. A few small doubts tried to worm their way into my subconscious, but I squelched them. This was his best idea yet, I told myself. A few glitches along the way provided me with some tense moments, however, and I upped my intake of antacids. Example: the clothes dryer move.

Some of life's riskiest ideas come to Idea Guys when they're home alone. My Idea Man decided he could single-handedly move our clothes dryer up sixteen basement steps with a little rope, a bit of muscle, and a lot of ingenuity. Then he would pop it into the back of his truck and deliver it to the new house.

Mr. Idea was marginally successful at first. All by himself, and with his own mental grit and brute strength, he got the dryer up to step number fourteen.

Bang. . .thump. . .bang. . .thump. . .bang. . .thump. . .

He stood there with the rope limp in his hands. The clothes dryer was back in the basement. . .not exactly upright, and not exactly in the same condition as it was on step number fourteen. Later he said it was like watching the dryer rappel down the steps in slow motion. He stopped to rethink his failed idea.

Idea Men don't quickly surrender to the possibility that some ideas aren't necessarily *good* ideas. His mind whirled as he stood at the top of the stairs, looking down on the dented dryer below.

What do I have to lose? The thing has already tumbled down fourteen steps. It doesn't look too bad.

After a few mental recalculations, he practically skipped back down the basement stairs. He wrapped the rope around the dented dryer at a different angle. Exhaling a loud grunt, he restarted his dryer hoist up the steps for round two.

"Voilà!" he declared when the dryer stood next to him on the landing. He got the still functional, slightly dented dryer out to the new house without another problem. Proof positive that Idea Men are as persistent as they are creative.

As we migrated to the country, I recalled the earliest biblical contrast between city and country living. God commanded Noah and his family to scatter and "fill the earth" (Genesis 9:1 NIV). When men decided some years later to build themselves a city so that they "*not* be scattered over the face of the earth" (see Genesis 11:4), the results were disastrous. It's safe to say country living is God's better idea.

After that brief biblical reflection, my logical conclusion followed: my Idea Man wasn't far wrong (if at all) to move us out of the city, even if the dryer did get a bit banged up in the process. That said, our move opened the gate for more ideas to flourish like the hybrid corn encircling us.

One night we sat curled up together, listening to myriads of crickets rub their legs together in a cacophony of country-style music. My Idea Man planted a tender kiss on my forehead and told me he had always harbored a secret desire. I raised a wary eyebrow.

"Oh?"

"I've always wanted to fly. Alone. We've got enough space for a hangar, enough land for an airstrip, and enough money to be financially creative. Why not?" he asked.

Before I could organize my thoughts into some kind of rational response, the Idea Man flew into action. The cricket concert forgotten, he went out and bought a kit to build his own airplane. Why—so went his thinking—get aboard a cramped and crowded plane with a bunch of other cramped and crowded passengers when you can build and fly your own aircraft in comfort and privacy?

He had never done this before. Nor had he ever taken flying lessons. He had no degree in aeronautical engineering and had probably never seen the inside of a hangar. Unlike his wife, he wasn't a Star Trek buff. But he had this idea that he could build a plane and fly it. He would build the ultralight aircraft first and take the flying lessons second. Such a simple, yet marvelous idea.

He built the aircraft, naming her *Harriet Mable* after his mother. I'm not sure his mother was particularly flattered, but the name was emblazoned in bright blue on the canary yellow airplane. *Harriet* (the aircraft, not my mother-in-law) taxied well under the command of the Idea Man on our grassy airstrip once he got her built.

When the time came, she flew well, too—with the Idea Man's flight instructor at the controls. The test pilot's words, after *Harriet*'s maiden flight, went something like this. . .

"You'll never get her up on your own," stated the seasoned pilot. My Idea Guy stood there grinning like a schoolboy. He had watched his creation take to the skies like a fledgling winging its way above the treetops.

"Nope," the flight instructor continued, "I didn't think I'd ever get her airborne. Too much plane, too little engine."

My Idea Man remained undaunted. He confided in me later, "*Harriet Mable flew.* That's the important thing."

Well, yes, he was right there. She did fly. After bumping and grinding across—not one, but *two*—large mowed fields and barely clearing the electrical wires strung along the road.

Wisely, my Idea Guy decided he should release his plywood and polyester pigeon to the bidding of an experienced pilot. Besides, he had begun to learn—with my gentle reminders—that this whole flying adventure had become one big money pit. Idea Men never lack for more ideas. Money, maybe, but not ideas. So my Idea Guy sold *Harriet Mable* (the aircraft, not his mother). He came up with a new idea: build a windmill.

I repeat, I am not making up any of this.

Power loss during inclement weather stalks

us country folk like a barn cat on the trail of an unsuspecting mouse. In a burst of genius, the Idea Man decided having our own power source would be a good idea. Maybe even a great idea.

"Why don't you just go out and buy a standard gasoline generator like most people do?" I asked foolishly. Wives of Idea Men do well not to ask those kinds of questions. The answers are convoluted and, in their own scary way, quite convincing.

Once the windmill dominated the northeast corner of our house, the huge, wind-powered, aerodynamic blades did us proud. My Idea Guy beamed with unbridled gratification when total strangers stopped their cars and asked with awe, "Is that a wind generator?" Such awe and admiration is very empowering to an Idea Man.

As it turned out, the wind generator wasn't a bad idea at all. An expensive one, but not a bad one. Time passed, however, and property taxes increased (the latter invariably follows the former). The Idea Guy decided to downsize. He didn't need the landing strip or hangar anymore, so it wasn't a hard decision to make. He disassembled the windmill and packed it up for our final move.

Just when I had begun to think my Idea Guy might no longer pursue any more unusual ideas, he surprised me yet again. Weeks before my birthday, he started to get almost giddy.

"I got you the perfect birthday present," he

confided. He couldn't contain his glee, so convinced was he that he had outdone himself. This, he told me, was probably his greatest idea ever.

My birthday arrived. With trembling hands, he handed me my gift.

"Here it is," he said, "the mother of all birthday gifts." He was serious, excited, and clearly proud. "Open it!" His eyes danced with anticipation.

I did. Stupefied, I looked down. I looked up.

"Well?"

I looked down again. Words failed me as I beheld the sight: the mother of all birthday gifts. His greatest idea ever.

My first handgun.

Me, who had never touched a gun in her life.

"We can go target shooting together!" he crowed.

Such has been the pattern of my thirty-plus years of life with an Idea Man. Sometimes it's been frightening. Like the time we almost had a northern Ohio prairie fire when he put a match to some dried grass and weeds. Sometimes it's been great fun, providing hours of entertaining videos. Like the time he almost drove the *Harriet Mable* into our living room. But those are stories for another time.

Yes, the guy whose name I took is more Idea than Ideal Man. Our story ends happily ever after. The last time I checked—after all these years of handmade aircraft and windmills and mind-boggling birthday gifts—we *still* don't have a bank account.

In your relationships with one another,

have the same mindset as Christ Jesus.

PHILIPPIANS 2:5 NIV

The Brick Baby

David McLaughlan

It was just a throwaway comment—if you believe in such things—but it led me to one of those moments that will warm my heart in my old age.

I was interviewing someone about a Spitfire aircraft that had crashed in a Scottish loch during WWII. The man I was talking to had been part of the team that recovered the wreck fifty years after it went down. He had lived in the area a long time. "If you want a good story," he said, "you should try and find some oot-by hurds. Their way of life is almost gone from memory now."

Oot-by hurds? I was curious, if confused.

"Hurds," he explained, were shepherds. "Oot-by" referred to the fact that they lived "oot" in the hills with their flocks, as opposed to the more civilized kind who lived "in-by" around the farms.

I had visited some of the tumbledown cottages in the middle of nowhere while hill-walking and had always wondered at the lives of the people who built them and the generations who lived in them. So I got in touch with a newspaper in the Scottish Borders area. They published my request and my phone number. It turned out the first folk to respond didn't live too far from me.

Sorn is a pretty village. You don't pass through it to get to anywhere; you have to actually seek it out. A few streets, a shop that also serves as a post office, a play park, and the remains of a castle on the hill. That's where Jimmy and Morag lived.

They were both in their eighties. Jimmy was a shepherd, the fifth generation of "hurds" in his family. Morag was the daughter of a shepherd and the wife of a shepherd. It had apparently been love at first sight when Jimmy's family had moved to a neighboring farm. He was fourteen; she was twelve. Neither of them ever looked that way at anyone else. Seventy-some years later, they were obviously still as much in love as ever.

They invited me into their home like I was family.

"Doesn't he remind you of. . . ?" Morag said, with a finger to her mouth.

"He certainly does." Jimmy answered her unfinished question.

"You look very like our boy," Morag explained. "He carries a bit extra weight as well."

Had I just been insulted? But something about this charming couple suggested they had never insulted anyone in their lives. Somehow their simple honesty completely disarmed me. I settled in like I was family.

All around the sunlit room were paintings and statuettes of border collie sheepdogs. When I asked if he ever got sentimentally attached to any of his dogs,

Jimmy dismissed them as tools of the trade—but it was obvious that many of them had found warm places in his heart.

In one corner of the room stood several shepherds' crooks with the ornate, curving heads he had carved from discarded rams' horns.

We chatted the afternoon away, and Jimmy gave me more than enough information and anecdotes to fill the article I was planning on writing. My favorite was when he talked about spending the night on the hills with pregnant ewes who were having difficulty lambing.

Now, even in springtime, the Scottish hills can still be snowcapped. In the middle of the night, with no shelter, they would have been bitter places to hang around.

Jimmy described how he would pull his collar up and pull his hat down. Then he would "hunker doon" beside the ewe. That way he would be right on hand if the ewe needed help.

"Must've been lonely at times, though," I suggested.

"Acht." He waved a dismissive hand. "It's a poor sort of fellow who can't put up with his own thoughts for a night. And when I got fed up talking to myself, I would listen to the Lord talk."

All the while Morag hovered near the side of her husband's high-backed chair. She would be adding to his stories, prompting memories, and going back and forth to the kitchen for tea, biscuits, or whatever else she could offer her guest.

I thanked them for a delightful afternoon and said I'd be in touch when the article was published. I got the feeling they were sad to see me go. Morag escorted me to the door. Jimmy wasn't too good on his feet.

Walking down the hall, her mothering instinct wouldn't let me leave without first asking if I wanted something to eat or drink for the trip home. Did I need to visit the toilet before I left?

I assured her I would be fine and said I had to pick up my daughter from school. I ventured that life for a modern six-year-old would be very different from Morag's childhood on the hills.

Now it was her turn to reminisce.

School had been fun. Of course it was a seven-mile walk to get there. There were maybe a dozen children in the whole school, and their homes were scattered all over the county.

Morag's home was so isolated her mother had once been cut off by snow for eight weeks while her father took the flock farther south. She just got on with raising her children and nursing her baby. There was nothing else for it, and it's what Morag's father would have expected her to do.

It used to be one of Morag's many chores to sweep the snow from the stream that ran past the front door, crack the ice, and bring in the water for the day.

Shopping was done once a month, and Morag used to look for her father coming back over the crest of the hill with the farmer's borrowed horse. He would be perched on the horse's rump, because the saddle would be laden with sacks of flour and the like.

The flour sacks, once emptied, would be bleached and filled with goose feathers to make pillows for the bed. Sometimes, if they had plenty of pillows, the sack would be made into underwear!

Living in the hills meant Morag didn't have many friends, but every once in a while her father would bring a sickly lamb in for her to nurse. There was one in particular she called Rosie. Morag would cuddle her and feed her from a milk bottle with a rubber teat. After Rosie was strong enough to rejoin the flock, Morag would shout her name as she walked past. A woolly head would always rise up from the crowd and reply, "Mehhhhhhhh."

"What about toys?" I asked.

"Oh, there was no money for toys."

Back then Morag's father was paid fifty pounds a year—and a pig! So luxuries like toys were scarce.

"How did you celebrate Christmas out there in the hills?" I asked.

"With prayers and hymns," Morag replied, and her smile brought a lump to my throat.

Different branches of the family would tramp

across the hills to gather in one cottage. Usually they would go to the house that had the youngest children. After all, a midwinter hike through snow could be tough on young legs or a mother carrying a child. Then, by lamplight, they reminisced, caught up, and praised the Lord.

The pig her father had been fattening all year would be butchered, and several families would be well fed over the Christmas and New Year period.

"It wasn't really about gifts," she went on, "it was about God and family. We might be given a sugar mouse and a piece of fruit. But, ohhh, one year I got hold of a catalog. There was a baby doll in there, and I wanted it so much. I was only six, after all! Well, of course, father and mother didn't have any money for such things. So father made me a pram from an apple box and some wheels, and mother wrapped a brick up in a baby blanket."

A brick? I wondered if she was kidding. I couldn't imagine any child these days being pleased with a brick for a gift. But Morag's gaze seemed to have left the here and now as she thought back across the years.

"Oh, I loved my brick baby so much, and I was as proud as could be pushing it up and down the road in my new pram."

Well, that story stayed with me. How could it not? I wrote it up and sent it to a Sunday newspaper. Not knowing if it had much chance of being published, I didn't think to tell Jimmy and Morag about it.

It did get published. But I missed it. The first I knew about it was when Morag phoned me a few days later. It seemed Jimmy had been taken to the hospital. It wasn't a serious problem but, because of his age, it meant an overnight stay for observation.

Morag had been at a loss. She'd been worried for her husband and couldn't remember the last night she had spent without him by her side.

Reluctant to go to an empty bed, Morag sat by the side of her coal fire with the newspaper, hoping it would distract her from the lonely ache she felt. She was surprised to find the story of her long-ago Christmas in print, but as she read it, the tale of her brick baby brought back the love and security of her childhood days. Her worries were replaced for a while by warmer, happier thoughts.

She slept soundly that night.

In fact she slept so soundly that she slept in. Rushing to get ready to go and visit Jimmy, she grabbed a handful of flowers from their garden to take with her.

"Oh, I was so embarrassed," she told me on the phone. "Imagine taking a sick man nothing better than a bunch of his own flowers as a gift."

But Jimmy had dismissed her bedside protestations. The flowers had done for him what the story of the brick baby did for Morag. Those crocuses with their stems wrapped in aluminum foil reminded him of home, a place where he belonged and where he was undoubtedly loved.

Well, Jimmy made it safely back home, and Morag got to fuss over him for a long time.

We kept in touch, and Morag kept me up-to-date with all the family news. She thanked me yet again for giving Jimmy someone else to tell his stories to. The magazine article did make it into print, and they both became local celebrities for a while. It was an honor to be able to do that for them.

All things pass. The days of the oot-by hurds are probably gone. Back then, Jimmy could give medicine to ninety sheep out of a hundred and come back the next day and pick out the remaining ten just by looking at them. These days, sheep are herded by men on four-wheelers and are electronically tagged. But the days of love look set to last a while longer.

Like most parents, Morag's mother and father did their best for their children, but their time was limited and their gifts perishable. No doubt the brick baby was laid aside and forgotten as Morag grew up and met Jimmy. But the love that took a brick and made it a cherished gift for a little girl proved much more durable than earthly things.

I doubt if her mother and father could ever have imagined their humble Christmas present would help their little daughter through a lonely night in her old age some eight decades later.

Since I first wrote this, Jimmy and Morag, the shepherd and the shepherd's wife, have gone to meet the Great Shepherd. But the memory of the brick baby and the love that warmed Morag's heart to the end of her days lives on, with me—and hopefully, with you.

"If you, then, though you are evil,
know how to give good gifts to your children,
how much more will your Father in heaven
give good gifts to those who ask him!"

Matthew 7:11 NIV

Imagine

Charles F. Miller

Have you ever been privileged? I don't mean the everyday sense of, "Thank you a lot, I sure appreciate that, that's terrific" kind of privilege; I mean cosmically, universally, heavenly privileged?

I am a nonmusician from a musical family. At St. John's Episcopal Church, in Royal Oak, Michigan, where I grew up, Mom and I would sit separately on the side—because everybody else in the family was up front making music. My brother is a terrific singer who married a terrific singer; my sister was a good singer and terrific organist and pianist, who was once chosen to accompany the Detroit Symphony. Mom and I. . . we couldn't carry a tune with a bucket and two hands! It's not that we didn't love to sing, but we were so bad we would throw the people around us off.

And then there was Dad. Dad had the best bass voice I ever heard, as well as being a mathematical genius.

But I get ahead of myself. Dad was born in 1913. He was a man of his generation. He could be gruff and stern; he didn't seem comfortable around small children, even his own. When we became teenagers, though, we found that he could also be very personable and even fun. But raising kids was the mother's job. He was a good father and worked very hard to provide. He was an accountant and an engineer. In WWII he was stationed at Pearl Harbor. He sometimes worked with the code breakers there on the secret Japanese war codes: the infamous "Code Purple." I'm sure that his mathematical skills proved very useful to those guys.

When I was in high school, Dad tried to help me with my algebra. But Dad and I are opposite. Physically, we're almost identical: 5 feet 11 inches, 165 pounds. Our brains, however, are exact opposites. I'm a poet; he was a math whiz. When he tried to help me with the algebra, it quickly became clear to me that while I was trying to figure formulas and rules on the paper, Dad was seeing the numbers. They were doing kind of a square dance in his mind—or, rather, in his imagination—moving into place almost as soon as he saw them. He couldn't help me. Our minds worked too differently.

Dad suffered from severe Alzheimer's the last nine or ten years of his life. For his last five years, the Alzheimer's was severe enough that he had to stay in a nursing home. But right up to the end, bits of him would shine through, including his mathematical acumen. He was still in the Detroit area; I live in Toledo. I visited him almost every weekend. One Saturday, when his Alzheimer's was quite advanced, I was wheeling him into the dining room. The classical radio station was playing from the ceiling. Suddenly, Dad blurted out a number, something like, "$446.34." I remembered the number and wrote it down. It was obviously the price of something. I asked him what he meant, and he of course couldn't answer. He didn't remember what he had just done. So I tried to remember what had just come over the radio. I vaguely remembered some sort of financial advertisement, with a popular local DJ as the voice. I figured that maybe the voice had given a price of something at, say, twenty percent off, and Dad had figured out the actual price. That would be like Dad.

So as I stayed with Dad through the afternoon, I listened for that ad again. It turned out to be an ad for a bank's home loan program. It gave a sample loan, something like, ". . .a fifteen-year loan for a $120,000 home is just 6.49 percent!" I wrote that down, too. I had to wait until I got home to test my theory about what Dad had done. I had a calculator with financial functions, and when I typed in the numbers my hunch proved correct, if barely believable.

In the space of about ten seconds, Dad—who didn't know exactly who I was, what year it was, or his own age—had figured out the monthly payment on that sample loan *correct to within a nickel*!

To this day I shake my head when I remember it.

I would take Dad out in his wheelchair during

good weather, and we would watch the cars driving along Twelve Mile Road, talk a little, and enjoy getting out. He could name some of the older cars. This was especially fun if there happened to be an antique car show going on somewhere near and the old cars would drive by or be taken by on trailers. The older the car, the more likely he could name it.

I discovered that next door to that nursing home is St. David's Episcopal Church. Dad was a lifelong Episcopalian; he became a deacon after he retired. One weekend I had the idea of taking him to St. David's for a service, thinking it would revive memories, thinking that he would probably remember the prayers and some of the hymns, all of which had been very important to him. He had always loved the Episcopal service. I called ahead to see if they could accommodate him. To my surprise, the deacon at St. David's was one of Dad's best friends. They had been right next door to each other for the last couple of years and hadn't realized it. The man was a few years younger than Dad, who was eighty-seven at the time. He and Dad had been friends in the same neighborhood and had gone to the same schools. They had both been on Oahu during WWII. Dad was in the navy, his friend in the army. They played golf together there, their units played baseball games against each other, and they had swum together at Waikiki. . .after the navy finally decided that there was no further threat of Japanese invasion and it was okay to take the rolls of barbed wire off the beach! This friend, an army officer, had even sneaked Dad—a navy enlisted man—into the army officers' club a few times. A rare treat.

I remembered this man and his wife as good friends of my parents after the war, back when I was a kid. And when Dad and I finally went to the church on a Sunday morning, Dad immediately smiled, laughed, and called his friend and his wife by their first names! It was the only time he would remember anyone's first name without prompting during the last five or six years of his life. I got goose bumps—and not for the last time.

As I've said, Dad had the best bass singing voice I ever heard, live or recorded. Those who had heard him earlier in his life agreed. And I mean *bass*. . .sub-basement bass. "Yes, he can hit *that* note" bass: resonant, clear, precise, and incredibly powerful at the same time. In all the singing that Dad did, I can never remember him using a microphone, and he sang in some pretty big places. St. John's was a cathedral-style church—the ceiling was three floors up there. But he never used a microphone. He could, however, also bring a song down to a whisper, and bring you to tears. While he was still in high school in Royal Oak, he had started singing the lead in local productions of light operas: Rogers and Hammerstein and the others of that time. He worked his way through two years at the

University of Denver by singing lead for the Denver Opera Company.

When I was young, we would go to a couple of Detroit Tigers games a year. We always sat along the first base line, and I'm sure, in the cozy little bandbox of Tiger Stadium, that his voice could be clearly heard by the folks sitting behind third base. For a while it kind of made me cringe. After I'd grown up a little, I stood tall and wanted to tell everybody: "You hear that voice? That's my dad!"

I've often thought that part of the grumpiness that Dad sometimes showed was because of frustration that he hadn't found a way to make a living with his voice, and with the acting that went along with it. I don't know if he even tried. It's just a theory. He certainly worked at his skill like a professional.

By the time he was eighty, when Alzheimer's started to show itself, Dad's voice was a shadow of what it had been, though you could still hear echoes of it at Christmastime or at church. He was never, however, off-key. As the Alzheimer's developed, it seemed to disappear. One of the problems he developed was an extreme difficulty swallowing. I figured that this had also put an end to his singing. The only thing he seemed to want to do with music anymore was listen to it.

So I didn't know quite what to expect when we went to St. David's. He surprised me a little by singing the hymns, or attempting to. He couldn't quite keep up with the rest of the congregation. He'd get the first part of the line out pretty well, but then he'd fall behind. He remembered the prayers of the service, too, but it was the same thing. He remembered them, or most of them, but he couldn't speak fast enough to keep up.

St. David's had an organist who was fairly well-known in classical music circles, judging from what he played at the beginning of the service and from what the bulletin said about his concerts. So I wasn't surprised when he started playing an extended piece after the service was over.

It was not a fancy organ piece. It sounded like variations on a hymn, though I didn't recognize the tune. It had the regular rhythm and melody of a hymn, and soon Dad was humming along—in harmony, of course. Then he switched from humming to kind of singing along by just going "Aaahhh-aah-aah-aaahhh. . ." When he did that, it sounded to me as if he had suddenly gone horribly off-key. My immediate thought was, *I guess Dad's finally lost it.* Then he'd go back to humming, and get back on-key. He'd do the hum for fifteen or twenty seconds, then the "Aaahhh. . ." for fifteen or twenty seconds.

Then I leaned over a little closer, because I couldn't really believe that those awful sounds were coming out of my dad. I listened more carefully. When he switched from humming to the "Aaaah-aah-aaaaah" singing, he was actually switching to the most exquisite, intricate, minor-key accompaniment imaginable, weaving it almost like a violin part around the major-key organ solo, almost like a bass equivalent to a soprano's "descant." It was as if he were taking the straight thread of the organ's melody and braiding, spiraling a minor key color around it like a helix of DNA, like the tracings of a ballet. It was mesmerizing. I have never heard anything like it, before or since. Suddenly, I was somewhere else.

Deep down inside my father, the musician was very much alive, maybe better than ever. Dad was in a place where he could be perfectly relaxed, with old friends, where he could be totally unself-conscious. Earlier, I had been given a glimpse through the fog of Alzheimer's into what his mind could do with numbers. Now, while he was listening to music as he had always loved it, I was being given a glimpse through the unself-consciousness of Alzheimer's into music as Dad had always *imagined* it.

This lasted for six or seven minutes, until the organ solo was finished. And I was the only one who could hear it. I got goose bumps. When it was done, I began quietly weeping at the pure privilege of being the one in the family who was honored to hear this. For a while, I couldn't bring myself to get up, grab the handles of Dad's wheelchair, and take him back.

If there is a heaven, this must be what music is like there, I thought.

But do you know what the best part is? When I describe this for people who knew Dad's love for music, people who heard him sing. . .

. . .*they believe me.*

"The kingdom of heaven is
like treasure hidden in a field.
When a man found it, he hid it again,
and then in his joy went and sold
all he had and bought that field."

Matthew 13:44 niv

Recycled Treasure
Kimm Reid-Matchett

There's an old saying that goes, "One man's trash is another man's treasure." My grandfather Charlie took that saying to heart. He saw great purpose in everything—from day-old doughnuts, which the town doughnut store would keep "just for Charlie;" to broken glass and rusty nails; to the wounded, broken-down people living on the wrong side of the tracks (or in his case, the trailer park across the road).

He would often make trips to the junkyard where he may or may not have been taking trash. Whether or not he left home with something in the back of his little red pickup, we could anticipate that he would eventually return with much more than he left with. Through his beautiful eyes, one of which was prosthetic and completely useless, he saw treasure in every pile of retrieved junk. My dear, sweet, and oh-so-patient grandmother Charlotte would just look out the window and shake her head, never saying a word about the sheds full of grandpa's "treasure" that were spread out along the back of their acreage.

One thing Grandpa Charlie grew especially excited over and would inevitably cause a sparkle to glitter in his one good eye was broken-down bicycles; it seemed like his yard was filled with them. Flat tires, twisted metal, plastic pedals, or ripped bike seats. Anywhere your eye might fall, there were sure to be bits and pieces of broken bicycles.

You see, Grandpa loved to see broken, discarded things come alive. He would get up long before the sun and begin tinkering with the broken pieces of bicycle. He would straighten the bent handles from one and lovingly put it on the unbroken frame of another. Adding patches and blowing up tires, sanding wooden blocks to replace the worn plastic pedals, he would eventually come up with a completely safe, albeit multicolored, usable bicycle. Once complete, he would set the newly revised bicycle over in the bike rack made from recycled, twisted lumber and rusty nails which he would tediously straighten—or get the grandchildren to straighten when they were showing signs of boredom—and smile.

If you paid attention, you would see him watching very closely. He wasn't concerned about the bikes being stolen. He purposely made the bikes for those children across the road who didn't have shoes, let alone bikes. Two or three of those kids would eventually wander into the yard knowing that my grandpa Charlie thought they were absolutely the best kids in the world and go directly to the bike rack. Walking around it and eyeing each recycled bike with precision and nervousness, the children would find one that fit them just perfectly—almost as if it had been made for them—and my grandpa would beam with joy.

My grandfather would then walk out from around the corner and gladly say, "Well I'll be jiggered, that looks perfect for you. I think you should have it!" Then he would help the child climb aboard and ride away. He became known throughout town for such treasures and often someone would drive into his yard with a couple of kids in the back and ask if this was the place where "my kids could get a bike." That would generally open the door for my grandpa to sit and smile and listen as yet another lonely parent would regurgitate a story of bad luck and hard times.

Eventually calling for the kids to come out of the backseat to choose a bike deeply blessed Grandpa; the parent would feel just a bit relieved as they received a firm handshake, often a bear hug, and the heartfelt words of "you come on back anytime." They usually would.

As time always does, it sped by quickly with Grandpa's eccentric ways remaining constant. The piles of treasure grew bigger and Grandpa grew older. One sad spring day, cancer caught up and grabbed tightly onto Grandpa Charlie. Not long after, we all gathered and heartbreakingly watched as a beautiful brand-new burial casket was lowered ever so gently and swallowed up by the earth.

The family chose to have a gathering the night

before his funeral where we could share stories and enjoy memories. The stories told were not of great wealth or who got his boat or vacation spots. He had none of that. No, the stories told were of his outrageous generosity with the little he did have— memories of his oversize heart and genuine love and compassion for everyone alike.

There were tears and sadness, but they were greatly overshadowed by the beaming pride we all carried out of the gathering that night as we realized how greatly we had all been affected by the model Grandpa Charlie had lived out before us.

When eventually we could face the fact that he was gone, nearly all fifty members of Grandpa's family got together for a work bee for the sole purpose of digging through sheds and returning most of his treasure to the junkyard where we all thought it belonged.

We still had failed to see through his eyes and now found it nearly impossible to find even the tiniest bit of value in the heaps of trash he had collected over the years.

Except. . .

The aunts picked up this or that and quietly stashed it into their cars to take home. I also noticed a few uncles pick up a tool or a can of screws that they'd stealthily throw into the back of their pickups hoping nobody was noticing that they were beginning to see treasure amid the trash. I, too, began to see through Grandpa's eyes, and the back of my van soon housed numerous treasures.

One of my most valued treasures from that day was an old metal bed frame, which I carted home and joyfully used for years. It was fantastically comfortable with the old-style springs and solid as rock because of the steel bars beneath holding it all together. A treasure to be sure!

Grandpa Charlie seemed to have an eye for treasure after all. The family used to enjoy teasing him, vowing to one another never to be like him and swearing we'd disown each other if, sadly, one of us did decide to see treasure in trash. We would roll our eyes and emphatically deny that the old man in the little red truck loaded up with junk was our grandfather. Today, we are proud he was.

What he unknowingly taught us was also deeply valuable and life shaping and Christlike. Grandpa Charlie taught us to see through the eyes of God. When others see junk, God sees value. In things, and more importantly, in people. All are made in the glorious image of God, and all are equally valuable to Him. Grandpa taught us—by example—to find that value in people, no matter what. To look for the down-and-out and simply love them.

Somewhere along the journey of my life and moving from one place to another, my dearly loved bed was lost. Actually, just the steel rods needed to hold the entire bed together were lost, making the bed useless. Because no one else saw the treasure that I saw, I was strongly and repetitively encouraged to get rid of it—return it to where it came from, the junkyard.

I'd likely not find the necessary bars ever again, so I gave in and sadly loaded it into the truck.

Many years later I stumbled upon a recycle shop where I could drop off things I no longer needed and could take those things I wanted.

I started popping in now and then to this wonderful recycle shop just for the fun of it. I began dropping things off, determined not to take things home. After all, it was junk. About the same time, my family was going through a number of hard times, finances being one of them.

Wandering around the recycle shop one warm spring afternoon, my eyes fell upon something—a treasure. I don't recall exactly what it was, but I remember whispering a very teary, "Thanks, Lord." I instantly had an overwhelming sense that God, maker of heaven and earth, the God who directs lightning and commands thunder, had just given me a special, well-thought-out gift.

I wouldn't always find a treasure, but every now and then—usually when I needed it most—He would surprise me with something or someone that deeply touched my heart. Every time His little presents would remind me that He is with me. His eye is ever on me, and He is aware of me. Better yet, He reminded me with these gifts that He knows exactly how to give me that message so that it will sink in and become meaningful to me.

I soon found that when I'd go out for coffee or milk or to pick up one of my children, my vehicle seemed to make turns I had not intended. Like a horse running to the barn, I'd find myself at the recycle shop. I would silently hope that the Lord had a treasure for me that day, like He had the day before, just so I could feel that exuberant sense of His care and love all over again. Whether He gifted me with a pretty item or a broken person, the feeling was the same— deep, supreme value.

Then one day there it was! As I was wandering around looking for a present for my father, my eye fell on what appeared to be a white metal bed frame. I gasped and excused myself from Patty, a wonderful treasure with whom I was chatting. I tried to walk nonchalantly toward the white metal frame, knowing full well I was half-walking, half-running, and looking like a complete idiot. I hoped I would get there before someone else saw this wonderful treasure and beat me to it. Turns out, nobody else was seeing through my eyes. I finally reached the prize. With crocodile tears streaming down my face, I stood there in almost unbelief as I ran my fingers so gently over my bed.

God is love and He loves me. . .and that day He went to extra-special lengths to make sure I heard Him telling me. Because Patty watched me act so silly over an old, scratched metal bed frame, I had to explain the story to her. I told her about my grandpa Charlie. I was able to share with her just how very much God loves us and what lengths He goes to just to show us His love.

I have my dearly loved bed back, and I am so excited each time I look at it or run my fingers along the cracked white paint or curl up in its soft, welcoming comfort. God Himself gave me a gift, knowing exactly how to tune in my ears to hear His voice. I also have a new friend who knows just how valuable God is, and how valuable I think *she* is, too.

While God gave me my bed back, He gifted me with a much more valuable treasure that day. He gifted me hope. He gifted me peace. He gifted me the unforgettable message that while I may be unaware of Him, He is always aware of me. He knows what touches my heart and is eager to do just that.

It never ceases to amaze me—the impact people can have on us without even intending to. I am forever grateful for the things my grandfather taught me. I know the Lord intimately because my grandfather genuinely loved the Lord intimately and encouraged me to do the same. I have an ability to see treasure in trash and the value in people because my grandfather chose to see through the eyes of the Father and taught me to do the same.

Thanks, Grandpa.

"His master replied, 'Well done, good and faithful servant! You have been faithful with a few things; I will put you in charge of many things. Come and share your master's happiness!'"

MATTHEW 25:23 NIV

A Guest Appearance
David McLaughlan

We tend to think of the story of our lives as *our* story. Sometimes, though, with the benefit of hindsight and a little emotional distance, we might look back and see the things we thought were all about us were actually more important as part of someone else's story. And maybe that's the way it should be if we are living lives of service.

This story, which I *thought* was mine, began on a rainy winter's evening in Glasgow, Scotland. Standing in Central Station, trying to get home to the coast, I looked up at the display boards and sighed as train after train was first delayed and then canceled.

I'd been waiting for over two hours to catch one of the trains that normally left every fifteen minutes. The problem was the rain. It was drumming off the roof of the train station, just like it had been all week. Higher level lines were fine, but the railway line that took me and hundreds of others home ran, in part, through a valley. In better weather the valley and the lochs in it were popular with local fishermen, but in wet weather (really wet weather) those lochs rose, burst their banks, and crept upward to the railway line.

Brave souls had been venturing out to the valley

each morning before the first train to see if they would be able to run a service that day. For those of us who had to get to work, the only option was to show up and wait.

Well, I'd gotten to work that day—but might not be getting back home.

Then they announced a train was going to try and get through.

Wrapped in the cocoon of the carriage, the journey didn't seem any different from normal. Once or twice we really slowed down but, looking out the window, all we could see was our reflections refracted in the rain and reflected by the dark.

We pulled into a little station in the middle of the valley. *So far, so good,* I thought. But the train doors didn't open. We just sat there. And sat there. Twenty minutes passed with no announcement. Then the lights went out.

Whatever problems the driver was having kept him distracted for another ten minutes. Then the doors hissed open, and he announced that this train would be returning to Glasgow. Anyone not wanting to return with it should get out now.

A trainload of people disembarked onto the plat-form. The station was unmanned; the waiting room was closed; people squeezed into the smokers' shelter. Those who couldn't get in were soaked in seconds.

I wasn't going to hang out. I decided to explore

the village beside the station. A few minutes later, I saw the lights of a taxi coming out of the dark. I waved him down. Could he take me to a little town called Kilwinning? It was about thirty miles away.

"Take you there?" The bear of a man behind the wheel laughed. "I was born there."

So I jumped in. On an impulse I asked him to drive past the station. Standing a little aside from the main crowd, I saw a young mom trying her best to shelter her baby.

"Where do you live?" I shouted out the window. It was a few miles farther down the road than me. "Jump in," I said.

"I don't have any money," she replied. "But I can pay when we get to my house."

Davie, the taxi driver, was a real chatterbox. It turned out he knew my folks. He talked all the way home while the young woman stayed quiet in the backseat. It occurred to me she might have thought she was taking a risk. Perhaps it was a measure of her desperation to get her baby home.

A mile from my place I asked Davie to pull over. I could get out at this junction, and he could take the woman and her baby straight on. It would get her home quicker. I gave him enough money to pay the fare for both of us.

He hesitated, then called me a gentleman and shook my hand.

Well, that's how it all began!

A year later I was married and going to a dance with my wife. Guess which taxi driver turned up to take us there—Davie. I didn't recognize him at first, but he remembered that night and spent the whole trip telling my wife what a righteous fellow I was. He recalled how the woman in the back of his cab had been busy with her baby and hadn't known what I was doing when I got out and how wonderful she thought it was to arrive safely home and find her fare already paid.

I tried my best to steer the conversation onto something else but, hey, it didn't hurt to have my wife know I was a gentleman even when she wasn't there.

The next time I met Davie, it was Christmas Day. A busy time for taxi drivers, and a time when they charge double fare.

Four generations of the family had gathered at my mother's house for a party. Near the end of the evening, we were all well fed and ready to put our feet up. But I had some young family members to get to the next town. I phoned a taxi, and Davie showed up. We wished each other season's greetings, and I gave him enough cash to cover the fare. When he dropped the youngsters off, he handed them the money back and said it was a Christmas present!

Time and again Davie was our driver. He would

insist on giving us a reduced rate. I would insist on giving him more than going rate. It was almost a competition to see who could be the nicest guy.

When he won the argument, I would put on a sour face and say I was going to phone a "real" taxi driver next time. But I never did.

On one of our trips together, I noticed Davie wasn't his usual chatty self. Oh, he still had that big wide-open smile—but it didn't seem to reach as far as his eyes. And there were actual gaps in the conversation. That wasn't like Davie at all. Something was up.

"Acht!" he said, waving a hand as if to wave the whole thing away. "It's just my mother. She's not very well."

I told him I was sorry to hear that. I'd heard Davie talk about his mom several times. He had an almost puppylike adoration for the woman.

"Actually, she's dying." Davie quickly brushed his cheek with the back of his hand. When he turned toward me, the smile was back—but I have never seen a smile so strained. "The doc says she has only days left."

I have no idea how we passed the rest of that trip.

This was a man I only knew in his workplace. But I felt I knew enough about him to know the heart of the man. We were really different guys in lots of ways, but I felt he had the heart of a servant, and I guess he thought the same about me. It was enough on its own to form a bond.

Well, I couldn't get Davie's mom off my mind. I managed to stall for a day, before remembering there weren't any days to spare. I swallowed my embarrassment and gathered my courage.

Davie had mentioned the sheltered housing complex his mom lived in, so I turned up at the reception area with a bunch of flowers. I was tempted to leave them there and run. But I didn't.

The oddness of the situation was reflected in the faces of the staff. Here I was, a guy turning up with flowers for an elderly lady I didn't know and hadn't ever met. I didn't even know her first name.

After checking to make sure it was okay with her, they showed me through to her apartment. A nurse took me into Davie's mom's bedroom.

Oh man, I was so not supposed to be in this lady's room—yet here I was, trying to undo the knot that had formed in my throat.

She looked up from the bed with an honest expression of delight on her face. I looked around the room, desperately trying to think of something to say. Everywhere there were signs of this woman's faith. And there were about a dozen vases full of fresh flowers!

I held my bouquet out and suggested she might have trouble finding space for it. The nurse took it from me and assured me she would find yet another vase.

"Isn't it beautiful," Davie's mom whispered, and I assumed she was talking about the flowers. "I'm going home," she added. And there was Davie's smile.

Well, I felt I ought to introduce myself. "I'm a friend of Davie's," I said. "Well, not a friend. A customer, perhaps." Then I told her the whole story. As I came to the end, I revised my introduction. "Actually," I said, "I *am* a friend of Davie's. He told me you weren't feeling so great. . .and. . .I just wanted to tell you that you raised a son to be proud of."

She seemed to think about this for a while, then she simply said, "Thank you." I stammered that I had better go now, but before I left I did a thing that amazes me even now. I stepped closer, kissed her on the forehead, and said, "God bless."

If I'd put my visit off much longer, I would have been too late. Davie's mom passed away the next day.

The task wasn't complete. There would be a funeral. Would it be too much if I showed up? The man was my taxi driver, for goodness' sake. Would he think it odd for me to turn up at his mother's funeral? Had he heard about the flowers? Did he already think I was weird?

These are the kind of thoughts that are planted in our minds to separate the good in our hearts from this world and the others in it.

Standing awkwardly at the graveside I tried not to be too conspicuous among a bunch of folk I didn't know. Then Davie arrived. Shaking hands and receiving condolences, he cut through the crowd and wrapped me in a bear hug.

He had been with his mum just before she died. And hadn't seen her so happy for a long time. She told him she'd spent her life raising her children, then, at the end of it all, a stranger came along and told her she'd done a good job. "What more," she asked him, "could a mother want?"

And he cried. And I cried.

But, really, it wasn't about either of us. That's the trap lots of people fall into, especially guys. We think our lives are all about us. But this story wasn't about torrential rain, it wasn't about paying taxi fares, it wasn't about which of us could be the nicest guy or the biggest gentleman.

This story was about a character who hardly featured. It was about a little lady who spent her life loving God and raising fine children; a lady who had done what she thought she was put on this world for, and done it with grace. Years in advance God had set a train of events in motion that put a nervous, confused stranger by her bedside to tell her the equivalent of, "Well done, thou good and faithful servant."

Looking back I now know all that stuff wasn't my story. But I am honored to have been chosen to make a guest appearance in *her* story. And, after all, it would not be the first time God has used a flood to arrange things just the way he wanted them.

And since we are his children, we are his heirs. In fact, together with Christ we are heirs of God's glory. But if we are to share his glory, we must also share his suffering.

ROMANS 8:17 NLI

No Princesses Here

Katherine Douglas

Congratulations! You have a new infant princess!"

The father of Princess Junko (pronounced *June-koh*) looked down on his tiny daughter. He wasn't born of royalty, but his wife was. Between his princess wife and his own important political position, Junko's future held promise. He beamed as she clenched his offered finger.

Here in the Japan of 1936, the new princess had the best before her! Born of royalty, political connection, and wealth, his infant princess would enjoy all the amenities available to one of her station. Junko's proud father could not foresee it, but his family's world would be transformed before she took her first steps—partly due to his choices.

—

"We're leaving!" Junko's father declared to his wife a short time later. "You will take my surname. Your father has pushed me too far!"

With that declaration, the lives of Junko and her family were forever altered. Before World War II, a man could take his wife's last name—and often did when marrying into royalty. When Princess Junko's parents cut ties with her mother's family, however, her father dropped the royal surname.

Now under her father's name, Junko's family left the royal ancestral home quietly and respectfully. All ties were severed between Junko's parents and her maternal grandparents. The toddling princess was too young to understand the rift between her grandfather and her father. Her mother did understand, and agreed with her father. Neither Junko nor her mother was ever called "princess" again.

Junko's father soon left politics, choosing to pursue a successful career in business. Junko remained the daughter of an important man, and she enjoyed a life of privilege. Over the course of the next several years, four brothers and two sisters enlarged their family. Unknown to Junko and her siblings, their father held a key position in the construction and design of a new kind of aircraft: the Japanese Zero.

—

"Watch me!" Junko shouted. "Watch this!"

Young Junko pushed off down the snow-covered hill, her bamboo skis tied securely to her feet. The home-made skis she and her friends wore gave them hours of winter fun. In the warmer months, Junko learned how to help prepare *mochi*, a tasty rice cake. On Girls' Day in March, pink mochi graced Japanese tables. White mochi filled up the table on Boys' Day every May. Japan's New Year celebrations meant lots of fireworks and boats decked out with arrays of candles. Junko's earliest school years were fun in her big family. Almost overnight, however, happy traditional holidays came to an end. Japan declared war on the United States in December of 1941.

Food shortages, fire bombings, and strafing runs obliterated carefree days of ice-skating, snow skiing, and springtimes making mochi. A day in 1944 encapsulated Junko's world of the mid-1940s.

"Run! Run for cover!" someone shouted, as the air raid siren screamed its warning.

In a panic, all the school children ran. Terrorized, Junko ran the wrong way—out in front of the *rat-a-tat-tat* of the warplane's machine gun. The loud drone of the low-flying aircraft, the deafening rapidity of the gunfire, and the puffs of sand around her couldn't make Junko run any faster than her eight-year-old legs allowed.

A sharp pain in her left leg forced a scream of pain from her. Before her legs buckled, a heavy weight from behind knocked her down.

Did the airplane hit me?

Dazed, her heart beating wildly, Junko couldn't move. Injured and breathless, she lay bleeding and trapped. The firing ceased, the warplane's drone faded, but Junko couldn't move. She realized someone—not something—was on top of her, pinning her to the ground.

"Please," she cried. "Please, let me up. I'm hurt."

No response or movement came from the crushing weight upon her. Her leg started throbbing. Bloody scratches on her face and arms stung. She gasped for breath. She heard running footsteps and shouts. With a grunt, a man rolled the unmoving man from Junko. Junko had multiple gunshot wounds in her leg, but the stranger had been riddled with bullets.

He died protecting me.

From that day until the war's end, approaching aircraft sent Junko running for cover. She never learned the stranger's name, but she never forgot him.

Junko's parents never spoke to her or any of her siblings about the bombings of Hiroshima and Nagasaki. As the war began winding down, her father was convinced horrible atrocities at the victors' hands awaited them. He planned accordingly, and one day made an announcement to the family.

"The war is over," he said during their meal one late afternoon. He looked at them, his countenance grave. Junko's skin prickled. "Japan was not victorious. The Americans and others will come here, and we must be ready to do what is best for us."

Junko and her siblings looked at each other.

What did that mean?

"If the occupying Americans ever come here," he continued, "we'll all eat this poison. Together." He hung a small bag of arsenic above their dining table. "It will be better to die together than suffer at their hands."

For three years Junko and her brothers and sisters never sat down to a meal without a furtive glance upward. Junko often wondered, *Will we have to eat it? What will it be like to die of poisoning?*

When her father read in the newspaper that they had nothing to fear from the occupying American forces, he took the poison down and disposed of it. The possibility of a family suicide pact vanished. Yet life for Junko's family changed again—dramatically and painfully.

Junko's father had to relinquish the money he'd made building military warplanes. He and his wife struggled to keep their house and land in postwar Japan. Junko's mother sold priceless traditional family kimonos to feed the family. When Junko graduated from high school, she could not have envisioned what lay ahead.

An early morning knock brought twenty-year-old Junko to her door grumbling. With eyes heavy with sleep and her hair in bright pink curlers, she pulled open the door.

"Come swimming!" her best friend invited her. Behind her stood two American GIs.

"What?" Junko demanded. "Do you know what time it is?"

"Time to go swimming! Look at the day! We'll have fun!"

"I don't know," Junko mumbled. "Besides, I can't swim."

"We'll just have fun at the beach. Come *on*," her friend pleaded.

After yanking the pink curlers from her long black hair and grabbing a towel and her swimsuit, Junko was introduced to her blind date. Her friend had been dating the shorter American for some time. He brought his friend, Alan, along for a double date. They thought a day at the beach would be fun. Junko wasn't convinced.

Her English wasn't the best, and this Alan spoke no Japanese. From what she understood, the American flyboy was from someplace in the middle of the United States. He had grown up on a farm and enlisted in the air force right after high school. Junko stifled a yawn. She should have just gone back to bed.

Fun? This guy can't speak a word of Japanese!

He was good-looking and muscular, but Junko found him irritatingly arrogant. She glanced at him again as they arrived at the beach and made their way along the shore. The way he carried himself. . .the way he looked down at her. He towered over her, so he had little choice but to look down.

Just the same, I'm not impressed, she thought.

Junko decided to make the best of the day for her girlfriend's sake. She could put up with this tall American for a few hours. Plus she could practice her English.

Junko and Alan walked into the water. She made it clear she couldn't swim, but walking in waist-high water seemed safe. She didn't want to drown, even if it meant deliverance from her date.

"Ohhhhhh. . . !"

Junko took a step and went down, down, down into a deep hole. She grabbed Alan by the neck. He had stepped into the same hole, however, and was quickly disappearing beneath the surface, too. The two of them did have something in common, after all. Neither could swim.

Alan grabbed Junko around the waist and threw her up and out of the water toward the shore. With all the savvy and unflappable dignity he could muster, he doggy-paddled his way out of the watery abyss to where Junko stood, blowing water out of her nose, her curly hair now wet and slick as a seal's.

Junko was neither grateful for nor impressed with her inglorious rescue. This. . *American* had manhandled her and thrown her up to the shoreline like a dead fish! And what kind of man invited someone swimming when he couldn't swim? She decided right then that she and the airman had had their first and last date. . .but, of course, they hadn't.

—

Junko soon learned that, like her, Alan was strong willed and opinionated. He liked a challenge, and found his ninety-pound, pink-curlered blind date as fun as she was challenging. They had gotten off to a bad start, but he didn't give up easily. He persisted, and three months later Junko finally accepted another date with Alan.

By their third date, she decided she liked this head-strong man. A year after their near drowning, Alan proposed.

"I'll talk to your father first, June," he said, using his name for her. "But I want you to think long and hard about this." He took her hand in his. "If he says yes, then I'll propose formally and expect your answer—yes or no. But I've got to tell you something." He hesitated, and Junko held her breath.

What's he going to tell me? Is there some shameful family secret?

"When my military time is done, I'm going back to Ohio. I'm just a poor farm boy, June. I don't have a lot of money, and never will. If you marry me. . ." He forced her to look into his eyes. "If you marry me," he repeated, "you'll probably never see your family—or come home—again. I want you to know that."

Junko nodded her head. She understood better than he knew. She loved him and smiled weakly.

But do I love him enough to leave everything and everyone I know?

Alan's meeting with her father was an all-evening affair just between the two men. Junko's father knew he would likely never see his oldest daughter again if she married the American. Alan knew he would be taking June where she knew no one and where no one he knew spoke her language. He also knew many Americans hated the Japanese people.

"Do you love him?" Junko's father asked her the next day.

Junko didn't hesitate. "Yes, Father. With all my heart."

"He's an honest man," her father said approvingly. He gave Alan his consent.

In 1958 Alan and June spoke their vows before the American ambassador in Tokyo. They spent their first months as newlyweds in Japan and believed getting June's green card to come to the United States would be a simple formality.

When they went to the embassy, they learned otherwise. With McCarthyism rampant in the United States, many Americans feared infiltrating communists. World War II wasn't that far from memory. Were any of June's family communists? Were any of them criminals? Would allowing June onto American soil pose a security risk?

June underwent a thorough and intimidating investigation, but finally her papers were all in order. With the arrival of 1959, she, Alan, and their infant son boarded their first airplane on the long journey to the other side of the world. Once they began flying over the continental United States, anxiety displaced June's excitement.

"We're *still* flying over the US?" she asked Alan after they had already spent hours over United States airspace.

"Yep! It's a big country!" he boasted.

June looked out the aircraft window again.

Does this country have no end? What have I done? Will I ever see another rice paddy? Taste mochi? She held their son tighter.

There are no princesses here.

Hearing and speaking nothing but English every day sometimes threatened to break June's spirit. Homesickness almost swallowed her up like the ocean hole on the day she met Alan. She longed for Japanese holidays surrounded by her family back home. But she had made her choice.

There's no going back.

Not until she was in her sixties did I know my Aunt June had been born a princess. After she related her story to me, I asked her, "What was one of the *best* things you remember about coming to the States?"

"Two things," she answered in her rich Japanese accent. "Your grandma and pork chops. 'Mom' welcomed me and loved me like a daughter from the moment we met." She grinned and a twinkle came into her eyes. "And I don't know how I ever lived without pork chops!"

The story of this Pork Chop Princess doesn't end with her never again seeing her family or the land of her birth. She and my Uncle Alan returned many times to Japan. And as for her native language? The former princess and her American flyboy watch her favorite Japanese television station daily in their air-conditioned Arizona home.

Dedicated to Junko (Hasabi) Takagi Halstead
(October 26, 1936–February 18, 2011)

"And the King will say, 'I tell you the truth, when you did it to one of the least of these my brothers and sisters, you were doing it to me!'"

Matthew 25:40 NLT

The Messenger

David McLaughlan

My grandmother was the daughter of Irish immigrants. The men of her family lived hard lives working in coal mines or the local iron foundry. As a relief from this poorly paid, backbreaking labor, they made regular use of the local hostelries and yelled away their tensions every Saturday supporting the local football team.

With six surviving children, a husband, and a widowed mother to look after—and very little money to do it with—Granny just got on with life. We kids never thought to wonder where she got her strength from. We would descend on her house every weekend assured of food, love, and freedom.

Many of our favorite childhood memories were gifts from her. They do say that I once paraded up and down the avenue in my diaper wearing her high heels, Sunday bonnet, and pearls! Grandpa was there and he was a good guy, but men of his generation didn't really play with children. Their contribution was working to make sure we were fed and had beds to sleep in. He used to tell us he would leave the house at five in the morning, walk two miles to the south, drop half a mile down a mine shaft, then walk two miles north again to the coal face. He joked he would be quicker sinking a shaft in his vegetable patch.

Twenty years after he died, part of his vegetable patch actually sank into the ground. A steady breeze blew up from that hole until the local council filled it with concrete. But before they did that I once watched Granny standing by the hole and gazing down. I wondered if she was now breathing the same long-buried air he had breathed all those years before.

Looking back it is obvious she found her strength in faith. Because she was the only one in the family who did, we kids tended to think that was just Granny's way. We never thought any more about it. She went to church every Sunday until her legs couldn't make the walk anymore. Then one of the congregation would take her by car. Then the minister would bring the service to her. We could see all this happen, but none of us got it.

When she finally went to her heavenly home, her grown-up children were distraught. There was no spiritual comfort from them. They just wanted to clear the house as soon as possible and get on. Very few mementos were kept. Practically everything was put out for the bin men. I guess it was just their way of dealing with the grief. She had been the rock their family was built on.

But on a rainy afternoon, three days later, her teenage grandson went back to her strangely empty house and searched through the trash cans. In the end

I came away with only two things—a soggy suitcase of family photos and her Bible.

During the next several years I made good use of those photos, copying them, printing them off for family events, and showing them to my own children. I used to leaf through the well-thumbed Bible and wonder what she got from it. But, I really had no idea. It didn't speak to me.

With Granny gone there was no faith influence in my growing up—and I didn't miss it. I was a rationalist, an intellectual. If there wasn't an explainable answer, then, as far as I was concerned, it was a dumb question.

My wife didn't think so, and I used to tease her for it. It was easy to poke fun at her faith. But then, isn't it always easier to criticize? Thankfully, she loved me more than I annoyed her.

On the train heading for an evening out in the city, I raised a subject I'd read about the day before.

"Is your church-going a substitute for Christianity?" Julie looked puzzled, so I explained. "It's about folk who claim to be Christian because they go to church every Sunday but don't actually live their faith in any practical way for the other six days of the week."

Well, we tossed the idea about for a few minutes. Sadly there are enough folk who live like that to make it a fairly easy target to hit. But, as Julie pointed out, faith is such a personal thing it's often hard to tell what it means to different individuals or how it affects their lives.

To be honest, I wasn't really that interested anyway. I was quite certain in my beliefs, and they didn't involve some big guy in robes floating about on a cloud. I wasn't looking for an answer; I was just passing time on a train and scoring some lazy points.

Then the train reached the end of the line. Once in the station we made our way through the masses of travelers toward the exit. You know what it's like; you focus on the people directly in front of you while others flow past on either side. All I was concerned with was getting out onto the street and finding a coffee shop before we went to the theater. The last thing I expected was to have my question put to the test almost immediately.

My wife tugged at my sleeve. "Look." She pointed through the crowd. I saw a bank of pay phones against the far wall. *So what?* I thought. Then I saw what she had seen. A hunched, elderly lady was moving from phone to phone, checking every change return slot.

Looking at her many layers of ragged clothing and shoes held together with silvery duct tape, Julie commented, "She's probably wearing everything she owns. And what she isn't wearing is probably in the plastic bag she's carrying."

I found a gap in the tide of people and stood for a moment, just watching her. Having found no forgotten change, this woman, who had to be in her eighties, headed for the newspaper shop.

She was so small I doubt the sales assistant ever saw her among the genuine customers. She picked up a magazine or two and "accidentally" shook out the advertising leaflets and free TV guides. She picked these up off the floor and tucked them into one of her many cardigans.

"Why's she doing that?" Julie asked. I could only guess they might be to help her through a cold night. I'd heard that crumpled paper stuffed inside clothes was a good insulator. But I'm sure it isn't anyone's idea of a cozy night. Maybe she rationalized that she wasn't stealing if she only took the stuff the newspapers gave away for free.

By now I was feeling like something of a voyeur. It was time to move on. I had seen poor people before. On the streets of Glasgow that night, I would probably walk past a dozen professional beggars. Life goes on. There was coffee and a show waiting for me.

But I couldn't walk away.

This was what I had been talking about on the train. How many of the folk walking past were churchgoers? But no one stopped to help. *How about you?* my conscience asked. *Are you any better than that?*

Well, I think of myself as a nice guy, but this was something different. There was a powerful urge keeping me there.

Once again the woman made her way, almost invisibly, through the crowd. Her next stop was the photo booth, where she pressed the coin return button a few times.

When she came out, I was standing in front of her. She stopped, but didn't really seem to see me.

"Find anything?" I asked. She jumped in surprise and looked up at me, her face a picture of confusion. She didn't seem to think I was police or security or railway staff. She didn't seem afraid. She just seemed totally confused by the fact that someone was paying attention to her.

What must it be like, I wondered, to live a life where being acknowledged is a startling experience?

"Here." I held out some money.

Her face ran through a range of expressions and her mouth moved, but the two seemed disjointed, out of sync. I had the distinct impression she was trying to remember how to speak. She shook her head, smiled, and her lips formed a silent thank-you.

Then it happened.

Stunned and scared, I stepped back into the crowd. By the time I reached my wife again, my tears were flowing freely.

Well, of course I told Julie what had happened,

but I didn't tell anyone else. After all, I didn't believe in that kind of thing. To believe the evidence of my eyes meant reevaluating the whole world I lived in.

A few weeks later, I went back to the station to look for that old lady. What I was hoping to prove by finding her I had no idea. It didn't matter; she wasn't there.

I went back the following week with the same results.

By the third week, I was beginning to wonder about myself. What was this obsession all about? Was I actually starting to lose my mind? Why else would I be stalking an anonymous bag lady?

Then I saw her. She was going through the same routine. I watched her check the phone coin slots, shake the inserts out of newspapers, and head for the photo booth. I followed her, not knowing what I was going to say, but hoping the transport police weren't watching me and wondering what I was up to.

I found myself in front of her for the second time, still not knowing what I was going to say. She looked up, curious, quizzical. "How are you doing?" I asked. She replied in a language that wasn't a language. I tried again. "Can I, maybe. . .help you with something?" There were more nonsensical sounds in reply.

And there was nothing there. The thing that had kept me coming back in search of her was nowhere to be seen. She was simply a confused old lady, living a hard life at the end of her days.

I pushed some money into her hand.

"God bless you!" I had never said that to anyone ever before. But my first meeting with this woman had hit my heart hard.

I'd thought it was enough to be a good man and do good things. I was kind of aware that it mattered how I lived my life—but that never squared with my "once you're dead, you're dead" philosophy. After teasing my wife about her faith, I tried to do a "meaningless" good deed and was immediately shown the meaning. I saw why it mattered.

If God, or His Son, had chosen to show Himself to me through that old lady, well. . .to be honest, I might not have recognized either of them. So, instead, He sent a messenger, someone I certainly would recognize. For a second or two that deeply lined, gray face and those watery blue eyes were replaced by a fuller face and emerald green eyes. It was a face I hadn't seen for over twenty years. It was the face of someone I still loved with the pure love of a child. My Granny.

And she was smiling. She was happy with me.

The tears are back as I write this, and I know, at last, what sustained her. I also know that her lifelong struggle was the least of her worries.

That old Bible I rescued from the trash sits on my shelf now. It's more worn now than when she used it. It speaks to me now.

Julie and I had been on our way to see *Jesus Christ Superstar* in the theater that night. I'm sure it was a good show, but I confess I only saw about half of it. The rest was blurred by tears of happiness.

And my God will supply all your needs according to His riches in glory in Christ Jesus.

PHILIPPIANS 4:19 NASB

Big or Small,
He Can Handle It All

Angela Deal

A heavy cloud hung over the church. The Barnett family's malicious rumors were spreading like wildfire, creating a ripple effect of confusion and broken relationships. My husband and I were caught in the cross fire because the Barnetts were our landlords. We were struggling financially, desperate for the acreage they rented to us, because it enabled us to park our thirty-year-old mobile home there while paying off debts. We simply couldn't afford to jeopardize our living arrangements.

But one day, when Mrs. Barnett had pushed too far, Romans 8:31(NIV) came to mind. *"If God is for us, who can be against us?"*

With a heavy sigh, I finally looked Mrs. Barnett straight in the eyes.

"No," I told her. "We don't agree with you." Then, after explaining my concerns, I said, "Look, Mrs. Barnett, I hope this doesn't destroy our friendship. But friends don't flatter. They speak the truth in love."

"How dare you!" Mrs. Barnett shrieked. "You're not a real friend." After spitting out several more livid words, she yelled, "We want you off our land!" Then she stormed off.

"Oh, God," I prayed, "what have I done? Please help!"

Suddenly, a gentle peace washed over me. *I will not leave you or forsake you,* God whispered.

With God's promises close to our hearts, my husband and I began searching for new living arrangements. But things didn't go so well. First, we hunted for a new location to park our mobile home on. But nothing was available. Either our mobile home was too old to put onto existing town lots or there were no other acreages available in the countryside. Then, when we tried getting a mortgage for a small house, rejection stared us in the face at every turn. Finally, when we searched for a house to rent, nothing was available in our price range. Before long, several weeks had flown by with no sign of help from God.

During that time, we decided to sell an old wooden grain shed that we had fixed up into a one-room cabin, along with a garden shed, a wood shed, a cattle shed, and some fence panels. We were hoping to bring in some extra money for our move, but, so far, we'd only received one response to our advertisements from a lady named Suzy.

"I'm very interested," Suzy said. "I just need to think about it. But, in the meantime, would you call me if anyone else shows interest in it?"

Since Suzy had been the only one to show interest,

and since I cleaned the office building where she was employed, I gave her my word.

"Yes," I promised. "I can do that."

Several days passed, but she never called.

My prayers turned from, "Thank You, God. I know You're helping us," to "God, where are You?" *Were all my prayers landing on deaf ears?* I panicked.

I found myself slipping into a dark hole of discouragement as waves of fear washed over me. Had God abandoned us?

I wonder which street corner we should live on? I'd mumble in self-pity.

I knew my simmering hostility toward our circumstances was destructive, but I couldn't shake my feelings.

Finally, I drove over to a friend's house.

"Carol," I said. "I'm sinking fast and I really need your help."

After explaining our dilemma, Carol smiled and said, "You know, it doesn't matter how big or small our problems are. God is in the business of doing miracles, and He can handle anything."

"Yeah, I know. But I've had serious doubts about that recently, and I've even told God so."

"Well, then, why don't we pray?" Carol suggested.

And, so, we did.

"God," I prayed, "I'm sorry for my rotten attitude and for losing faith in You. Please help me to trust You again."

When I finished, Carol took over.

"Lord," she prayed, "please encourage Angela today. Show her that You are still in control and that You haven't forgotten about her. Please do a miracle for her family."

Fireworks did not explode. We'd just reached out to God in simple prayer, so when I climbed into my car to leave, I never imagined the lengths God might go to in answering our prayers. Though discouragement still loomed heavy over me, I felt better because I'd sought and found God's forgiveness for my sour attitude. And that really helped.

As soon as I arrived home, I hit the PLAY button on my telephone answering machine. There was one message.

"Hey, my name is Victor," the message played. "I'm interested in your cabin. Please call me."

"Wow!" I gasped. "This is good news."

Immediately, I phoned Suzy but only got her answering machine.

"Suzy," I said into the recording. "There's someone else interested in the cabin, so I need to know if you're still interested or if I should proceed with this guy? Please call me right away."

I hung up. Then I phoned Victor and explained my circumstances to him.

"Hey, that's not fair!" He griped. "You should sell it to the first person who pays you."

"You're probably right," I said, "but I need to

honor my word with her. After all, I clean the office building where she works, so I don't want to create waves with my job."

"Oh, all right," he mumbled. "But can I still look at it in the meantime?"

"Certainly," I answered.

Moments after I hung up the phone, another call came through.

"Hello?" I said.

"Hello, this is Harry. I'm interested in the cabin you have advertised. I'd like to come see it."

Puzzled, I rubbed my temples. *Another call about my cabin?*

"Sure, Harry," I said. "You're welcome to come see it, but there are two other people interested in it right now."

Harry took down the directions to my place anyway, and we hung up.

Fifteen minutes later, my daughter called. "Mom, someone just drove into our yard."

"That must be Victor," I mumbled. I walked outside and found a short, heavyset man with small, round glasses framing a balding head. I showed him the cabin.

"Yes, I like this," Victor nodded. He wandered around the outside of the cabin, then stopped and stuck a dull knife into a piece of the trim.

"Aw. . .see, this means wood rot."

"Actually," I responded, "that doesn't reflect the rest of the cabin, because it's just an old piece of wood my husband used to replace part of the original trim."

"Well, you should go down in price," he muttered. "See what Suzy wants to do then let me know, okay?"

I agreed. He left.

I walked back into the house to see if Suzy had phoned. Still nothing. So I left another message on her answering machine.

"Suzy, please call me right away!"

When I hung up the phone, another message waited for me on my answering machine.

"Hi, my name is Ray. I just saw your ad for the cabin. Please call me back."

I called Ray and explained my dilemma.

"Oh, that's a shame," he said, disappointment ringing in his voice. "But, hey, will you let me know what Suzy decides?"

"Sure," I answered. We said good-bye.

"Mom! Someone else is here!" my son hollered this time as a plump, blond woman wandered toward the cabin.

What's going on here? I wondered, heading toward the door. *Why all this sudden interest in my cabin?* Before I could slip out the door, the phone rang.

"Mom, it's for you."

I rushed back. "Hello?" I answered.

"Hi, this is Suzy. Sorry I never got back to you sooner. Unfortunately, I can't buy the cabin after all."

"Well, finally! If only I'd known that from the start," I muttered under my breath. After saying good-bye to Suzy, I scurried out the door to find the blond lady, but she had disappeared. I stood there shaking my head, baffled. Finally, I retreated back into the house and phoned Victor.

"Okay, Victor. I just heard from Suzy. She's not buying the cabin after all."

"Great!" Victor rejoiced. "I'll take it off your hands for half price."

"Whoa!" I said. "That's too low."

"Well, that's crazy!" he sneered. "You're not going to get a better offer than that."

"Well," I told him. "I'm sure going to try."

We said good-bye, and I laid my head down on the table.

Oh, God, please help me!

Suddenly, I remembered that I was supposed to call Ray, so I scurried over to the phone and dialed him up.

"Hi, Ray. Suzy isn't buying the cabin after all, so you're welcome to come see it."

"Oh, that's wonderful!" he exclaimed. "I'll be right over."

Twenty minutes ticked by and my son called again. "Mom! Now there's a man outside."

I dashed out the door. "Hi, you must be Ray?"

"No, I'm Harry," he answered. "Why? Is someone else coming to look at the cabin?" Harry's eyes grew large and frantic, and I had to fight from laughing because with his thick, disheveled head of brown hair and short, bushy beard, he looked like a wild jungle man.

"Well," I paused. "Yes, there is."

"Oh, no!" Harry wailed. "My boss sent me here. She was here earlier but left to go get her husband. She wants the cabin."

Good grief! I panicked. *How was I to know? The woman left without saying anything, and now I've invited Ray to come see it.*

Suddenly, a white truck turned onto our graveled driveway.

"Is that your boss?" I asked Harry.

Harry's eyes grew even larger. "No!" he gasped. "That's the other guy, isn't it?"

"Uh, I guess so." I winced.

In a rush, Harry grabbed his cell phone and punched in a number. Then he reached for a wad of money and shoved it at me. "Take this," he pleaded.

I stepped back without taking it. *I'm no salesman!* I screamed in my head. *Shouldn't Ray at least get a chance to see the cabin since I invited him to come?*

Clutching the phone close to his ear, Harry muttered to himself over and over again. "It's mine, it's mine. I was here first."

Oh! If only I could escape this madness.

When Ray climbed out of his truck, I led him to the cabin while Harry looked on in horror. My legs felt weak.

"I'll be in the house if you have any questions," I told Ray in a shaky voice.

Somehow I made it through the door and collapsed into a soft, velvet recliner. *What's going on here? Why has this place turned into a madhouse?*

Moments later my daughter said, "Mom, there's a guy at the door."

With unsteady gait, I walked to the door and found Ray standing there with checkbook and pen in hand.

"I'd like to make an offer," he said, giving me an amount.

Oh, Lord, what do I say? Several seconds of awkward silence went by before I found my voice. "Oh, Ray, I'm sorry. I just don't know what to do. You see, as you were driving into the yard, that man out there was frantic. He tried shoving money at me to reserve the cabin until his boss arrived, but I didn't take it because since I invited you over I figured you should at least be given a chance. I thought after seeing it, you might not be interested. Now, I'm at a loss what to do!"

Ray smiled. Oh, how I needed that! "I'll tell you what," he said. "Let Harry make an offer, then you can sell it to the highest bidder."

I took a deep breath. "Thank you," I said in a voice barely audible.

We walked outside. Ray joined his wife and daughter on one side of my sidewalk. Harry, now joined by his boss, her husband, and their two teenage kids, stood on the other side. When I noticed eight pairs of eyes staring at me, I stopped, frozen in my tracks. *I can't do this!* I cried inwardly. My jaw fell open, but no words came out. Suddenly, the crowd roared with laughter.

"You poor girl," someone said. "Bet this has never happened to you before."

I burst into laughter then, too. "No, it hasn't."

Finally, I looked at Harry and said, "These guys made an offer, but I'll give you a chance to make one, too. Then the highest bidder can have it."

"We'll pay the full asking price," someone from Harry's group piped up.

I glanced over at Ray. "That's all right," he smiled. "Let them have it."

While Harry's boss wrote me a check and made arrangements for pickup, Ray wandered around the acreage. When Harry's group left, I walked over to Ray.

"Are you selling your garden shed?" he asked.

"Yes," I answered.

"Well, I'd like to purchase it plus your other buildings and fencing."

After Ray left, I sat down on an old log, stunned. *How could so much happen in one afternoon? A hard-to-reach woman, a pompous man, a mysterious woman, a crazy guy, a gentleman, and a clueless saleslady. What a comedy act!* I shook my head in disbelief. Suddenly, a firm yet gentle voice boomed into my thoughts. *NOW DO YOU BELIEVE I CAN STILL MAKE MIRACLES HAPPEN?*

I turned but saw no one. Then as a rush of warmth surrounded me, a smile broke across my face.

"Oh, yes, God, I do!" I laughed. "Thank You for showing me that You really are still in control."